From the Beginning

WHAT OTHERS ARE SAYING...

I found *From the Beginning*, by Eric and Carol Smith to be an awesome addition to the on-going discussion of the role of women in leadership in the church today. It is a book that has a tone of humility, but is also filled with decades of doing ministry together as husband and wife. They have made careful inquiry into many of the difficult passage in the Bible related to this significant subject. Reading *From the Beginning* was not only a great adventure through the rare work of a husband and wife team, but a clear explanation of their position as biblical egalitarians. I highly recommend this work to any and all who are interested in seeing the church become more relevant and effective in our world today.

— STEVE CLIFFORD
Lead Teaching Pastor
Westgate Church, Silicon Valley

This book is written with humility and power and is a timely call for freedom. I'm convinced an empowered future for women is deeply connected to the advance of the Gospel and the equipping of the church. Eric and Carol Smith do an incredibly thorough job of Truth telling, offering a tapestry of Biblical exegesis, theological insights, practical experience and personal conviction. This book will help us all move towards Jesus' best plans for the redemption of all things.

— DANIELLE STRICKLAND
Speaker, writer, activist
author of *The Liberating Truth:
How Jesus Empowers Women*

What good news that we get to live in this season of church history – a season of repentance. The Christian church is waking up to ways that we have misunderstood, misapplied, and misused our own Bibles regarding women and men in ministry together. I'm so grateful to Eric and Carol for writing this book to help us all become more of the Church God intended us to be.

—BRUXY CAVEY
Teaching Pastor at The Meeting House
author of *The End of Religion and (Re)union:
the Good News of Jesus for Sinners, Saints, and Seekers*

From the Beginning

A Biblical Response to Christian Patriarchy

Eric Scott Smith | Carol Nelson-Smith

You Define Us Press

Copyright © 2020 by Eric Scott Smith and Carol Nelson Smith

All rights reserved. No part of this book shall be reproduced or transmitted in any form or by any means, electronic, mechanical, magnetic, photographic including photocopying, recording or by any information storage and retrieval system, without prior written permission of the publisher. No patent liability is assumed with respect to the use of the information contained herein. Although every precaution has been taken in the preparation of this book, the publisher and author assume no responsibility for errors or omissions. Neither is any liability assumed for damages resulting from the use of the information contained herein.

All Scripture quotations, unless otherwise indicated, are taken from the Holy Bible, New International Version®, NIV®. Copyright ©1973, 1978, 1984, 2011 by Biblica, Inc.™ Used by permission of Zondervan. All rights reserved worldwide. www.zondervan.com The "NIV" and "New International Version" are trademarks registered in the United States Patent and Trademark Office by Biblica, Inc.™.

Scripture taken from *The Message* Bible translation is copyright © 1993, 1994, 1995, 1996, 2000, 2001, 2002. Used by permission of NavPress Publishing Group.

ISBN 978-0-578-64888-0
You Define Us Press

Contact authors at **www.youdefineus.org**
Book Cover designed by Charlote Licayan (Relic 88 at **www.99designs.com**)
Book and E-Book designed and formatted by
www.ebooklistingservices.com

Publisher's Cataloging-in-Publication Data
Names: Smith, Eric Scott, author. | Nelson-Smith, Carol, author.
Title: From the beginning: a Biblical response to Christian patriarchy / Eric Scott Smith ; Carol Nelson-Smith.
Description: El Dorado Hills, CA: You Define Us Press, 2020.
Identifiers: LCCN: 2020902887 | ISBN: 978-0-578-64888-0
Subjects: LCSH Patriarchy--Religious aspects--Christianity. | Sex role--Religious aspects--Christianity. | Women--Religious aspects--Christianity. | Women in Christianity. | Men (Christian theology) | Families--Biblical teaching. | Marriage--Religious aspects--Christianity. | Equality--Religious aspects--Christianity. | BISAC RELIGION / Christian Living / Family & Relationships
Classification: LCC BT706 .S65 2020 | DDC 270/.082--dc23

Printed in the United States of America

DEDICATION

This book is dedicated to our readers, who like us, are in search of a fresh understanding of what biblical manhood and womanhood really looks like. It is a call to greater freedom for both men and women who believe there should be a fuller expression of what it means to be created in the image of God. Thank you for joining us in rethinking the roles of men and women in both marriage and ministry. Our prayer is that this book will encourage and empower you to move forward in serving God with a greater sense of confidence to be who he made you to be and to serve him without man made limitations.

Eric and Carol Smith

TABLE OF CONTENTS

Introduction..1
  Reclaiming Biblical Manhood and Womanhood

PART I
RETHINKING PATRIARCHY
IN THE CHURCH

Chapter One...13
  Christian Patriarchy, an Oxymoron?

Chapter Two..23
  Closer to Home

Chapter Three..37
  The Very Best Scenario

Chapter Four...47
  But Isn't God Male?

Chapter Five..59
  When Good Goes Very Bad

Chapter Six..67
  Opposing Desires

Chapter Seven...77
  The Fallen World Social System

PART II
GOD'S STORY OF WOMANHOOD

Chapter Eight..87
    The Weaker Vessel

Chapter Nine...99
    Taken by Surprise

Chapter Ten..111
    God-Sanctioned Authority over Man?

Chapter Eleven..121
    A Game-Changer for Women

Chapter Twelve...139
    Women Beyond the Cross

Chapter Thirteen...147
    Women in the Early Church

Chapter Fourteen..159
    The Church Gets Off Track

Chapter Fifteen...169
    The Early Women's Movement

PART III:
OPENING DOORS CLOSED TO WOMEN

Chapter Sixteen..183
    The Eye of the Beholder

Chapter Seventeen..191
    Turning a Blind Eye

Chapter Eighteen..203
    The Silent Treatment

Chapter Nineteen..213
    A Red Flag

Chapter Twenty..223
    For Better or For Worse?

Chapter Twenty-One...233
    Two Words Say It All

PART IV
WHO HAS COMPROMISED?

Chapter Twenty-Two..247
    The Things That Matter

Chapter Twenty-Three..253
    What's the Point?

Epilogue..263
    Setting the Record Straight

About the Authors..267

Acknowledgements

This book would not have been possible without the support and encouragement of:

Marie and **Brenda** for helping me (Carol) to believe in the value of "my story."

To our editor, **Jeannette Windle** who saw greater potential in this project than we would have imagined.

To my (Eric) friend and confidante, **Steve**, who faithfully read through four revisions of our manuscript.

To **Jeff** who courageously gave us honest feedback.

To **Bruxy Cavey**, pastor of *The Meeting House*, for his out-of-the-box perspective that gave us eyes to see beyond traditionalism.

To **Marge Mowczko** for daily inspiration provided by her years of blogging for women's equality.

To **Steve Clifford**, Lead Pastor of Westgate Church, Silicon Valley, for his courageous decision to open doors of church leadership to women.

To **Danielle Strickland** whose life and ministry inspired me (Carol) to see the potential of women as influencers and leaders in God's Kingdom.

To **Christians for Biblical Egalitarianism** for representing the cause of women for so many years with the hope of building a better and stronger church.

To **Debra** who encouraged me (Carol) through the first, very rough draft of the manuscript when this project was still in infancy.

To **Liesbeth** whose regular inquiry about how the book was going encouraged us to see this project through.

To **Connie Trouard** for sponsoring the printing of our book for distribution in Africa

To our children **Eric**, **Rachael** and **Toya** (and their spouses) for loving us through challenging times.

From the Beginning

Introduction

Reclaiming Biblical Manhood and Womanhood

Today's heightened awareness and unrest in the global crisis of gender discrimination and injustice is signaling a need for re-evaluation and change in the church. Abuses of male superiority in ministry and marriage are being exposed as just the tip of an iceberg. Marriage based on an authority structure giving men greater power has proven an inadequate foundation for stability and intimacy. A growing number of church leaders affirm that alleged prohibitions regarding women in leadership do not have the clear support of Scripture as historically claimed. Those promoting these prohibitions do not have the final word. Much more needs to be said about gender bias in the church and the misrepresentation of God's first and final word on this subject.

Many are catching a fresh vision for womanhood and manhood that more closely expresses God's heart as revealed in Scripture. Women are coming out of the shadows cast by what we believe to be inaccurate interpretations of Scripture to find their voice of leadership in the church. God is calling men and women to partner together in leading the way to greater spiritual life, liberty, and justice for all.

A movement among many sincere believers, characterized by mutuality and shared leadership between men and women in the Christian community, is courageously questioning the biblical basis prohibiting women in leadership. Is it really God's intention for the church and its ministries to have a masculine feel? Should gender or calling and gifting be the determining factor of what one is permitted to do in the church and in the marriage relationship?

We (Eric and Carol) have found that most believers are unaware of the magnitude of the debate taking place regarding the roles of men and women. The challenge to understand the heart of this debate shouldn't be limited to pastors and church leaders since the outcome personally impacts the lives of millions of believers around the world. This dialogue needs to be taking place in Christian homes, small group Bible studies, and wherever believers gather.

As co-authors of this book, we have a vision for renewal in the church. We believe the traditional teaching that opposes a woman's calling to leadership within the church doesn't line up with God's original design for manhood and womanhood. We hope to show this by presenting a fresh look at Scripture unclouded by traditional presuppositions.

As a pastoral couple who both have strong leadership gifts, we've struggled personally to reconcile our roles within the traditional model of ministry and marriage. By candidly sharing our challenging journey of nearly five decades and the surprising biblical discoveries along the way, we hope to encourage husbands and wives, pastors and church leaders, and believers in general to bring this controversial issue to the table for more open and honest discussion.

Our Journey

Let us start off with a quick snapshot of our backstory. We are both life-time Californians. We were both born in 1950 and attended the same high school in the San Francisco Bay area, although we didn't meet until the fall of 1969. We were nineteen when our paths crossed at De Anza College in Cupertino. Both in search of purpose for our lives, we found it together by joining the Jesus People Movement. For those unfamiliar with this renewal period, this movement was a response to the church's ineffectiveness in addressing cultural unrest among the youth at that time.

The Jesus Movement began in the late 1960s on the west coast of the United States, from where it spread through North America, Europe, and Central America before largely disbanding by the late 1980s. Members of the movement were called Jesus people or Jesus freaks. Our own Jesus freak days, living in Christian communes, passing out tracts at anti-war rallies, and preaching on street corners and college campuses, were charged with a passion to model Jesus's mission of love and hope to our disillusioned generation.

The meta-message driving the intensity of this movement was a challenge for change within the church. A wake-up call to get its head out of the clouds and become more relevant. These formative years set a trajectory for our ministry that would not be afraid to challenge the status quo of traditional "churchianity." Married in 1971, we found a church home that fit our out-of-the-box convictions. Soon after, we registered to attend Bible college and were hired by our church to start an outreach ministry.

We served in that church for the first twelve years of marriage, then moved to Gilroy, California, to pioneer South Valley Community Church, a new non-denominational church. We ministered there for thirty-one years before transitioning church leadership to a younger team anxious to serve their own generation with a fresh vision. We never thought much about what retirement would look like until it happened. Now no longer responsible for the day to day operations of the church nor in the spotlight we suddenly had fewer demands and more time on our hands than our entire married life. While an unexpected void, this also gave us opportunity for personal reflection and re-evaluation of a life together that had been marked by our fair share of difficulties.

It is now nearly fifty years since we first made a commitment to serve God together. Looking back, we thank God that our commitment to each other survived despite years of misunderstanding God's design for marriage and ministry. What we are going to share about our personal journey is what we wished someone had taken time to share with us.

Despite my (Eric) unconventional approach to ministry, I'd been committed to the church's traditional view that limits women in leadership. My upbringing in a full-blown dysfunctional family left me with a shaky foundation for my own sense of security as a man. My father was an angry alcoholic who died at an early age, leaving me to be raised primarily by my mother. In tandem with my brokenness and sinful nature, I found it easy as a pastor to accept patriarchal teaching on women's submission to men. Teaching that conveniently gives pastors authority over more than half of their congregation.

Married to a Gifted Woman

The irony was that I'd married a woman with strong leadership gifts I didn't have and that I recognized our church desperately needed. The doctrinal position I'd taken automatically disqualified Carol from positions of leadership and set limits on her influence. I found myself being duplicitous, embracing Carol's gifts when I needed them while feeling justified in rejecting them (and her) when I felt threatened or intimidated. This created all kinds of frustration for Carol and tension within our marriage and church. It was like giving her just enough rope to hang herself, and that was true of other strong women in our church as well.

On several occasions, I was confronted with my inconsistencies and the consequences of the traditional position I'd taken. I coped with the issue by basically ignoring it, doing my best to keep the peace and pacify the agitators while hoping it would just go away. I now regret allowing my own apprehension to minimize the problem and marginalize women from participating in influential positions of church leadership. I also feel compelled to apologize for my erroneous assumption and the sinful attitudes that kept me from being more honest.

One significant motivation for revisiting this critical issue stems from my conviction that by rejecting women in leadership the church has robbed itself of half of the image of God. I believe one reason the church has been anemic and ineffective can be traced to its discrimination against women. Far too often men have been willing to use women in roles to help them look better and cover their incompetency. We willingly send women off as missionaries to deal with the hardships of living in developing countries and even risk their lives while never offering them a seat at the table of genuine spiritual leadership in the church.

As a result, both men and women have suffered greatly. Women because they've been denied the opportunity to fulfill their God-given calling, and men because they've been forced to assume aspects of leadership for which they were not qualified. As a pastor, I have repeatedly witnessed the ineffectiveness of this male-dominated leadership model. The duplicity of the church has clearly been detrimental to a proper understanding of the Gospel and its influence on society. It has handicapped the church from being a living witness of the complete image of God to a watching world.

I (Carol) would like to jump in here to give my husband an enthusiastic high five for his courage and integrity in sharing his convictions. His tenacity in reading and studying for months on end before arriving at the conclusions he'll be sharing is beyond admirable. I have watched my husband painfully wrestle with the scriptures we were told closed the door on women in leadership only to discover their faulty premise. I couldn't be more thrilled to be experiencing this transformational truth that has brought renewed vitality in our relationship.

This book was originally to be about my harrowing adventures in the nebulous land of Christian womanhood as a pastor's wife. The early title we'd chosen was *The Bride with a Man's Voice and other Detractors on the Feminine Journey*. That name got shot down by our editor's concern the title suggested either gothic horror or transvestite fiction. I got a good laugh when I read her review, but I'm still a bit attached to the original title as it represents my personal struggle and the daunting questions that launched this project and kept us going to the finish line. It also begs the answer to a very important question. If the church is referred to in Scripture as both the body of Christ and the bride of Christ, highlighting its dual male and female nature, why has "she" been given only a male voice and assigned a masculine feel?

Although in creation God's image was expressed as both masculine and feminine (Genesis 1:27), I found that hard to envision growing up in my church as a child. While manhood and masculinity were clearly validated and showcased both inside and outside the church, I was left questioning what value God places on women. Ultimately, it was in discovering a more complete biblical perspective that brought me to a place of reconciliation with womanhood as designed by God and not assigned by men.

Disconnected from Myself

Until that happened, my journey was marked with a pronounced sense of disconnect with the portrayals of womanhood in our male-dominant culture, the church not excluded. I was raised in a very conservative Christian home and from a young age observed the disparity of what it meant to be a girl and not a boy. Early on, I learned that God was a "he" and not a "she." As our heavenly Father, he sent his son Jesus to earth. Jesus chose twelve men to be his first apostles, and most of the Bible heroes I learned about were stories written by men about their adventures with God. It was always men who gave the talks on Sunday mornings. And they talked primarily about God choosing other men whenever there was something important to be done. The message spoke loud and clear. Men matter more than women.

Probably not unlike most of us, I grew up with an intense need to be someone special. I also had a strong inclination to be a leader but had some irreconcilable questions. As a woman what was being a leader supposed to look like if men were given the authority and leadership roles in both marriage and in church? Over the thirty-one years we served in our Gilroy church plant I can't think of any ministry in which I wasn't involved, including international missions. As I sought to understand what was acceptable for a woman to be and do within the Christian community, I found there were things about me that were met with disapproval. I now understand this isn't unusual when a woman with strong leadership gifts tries to find her place within the male-dominant culture of the church.

As Eric's wife, I was included in leadership roles beyond the traditional church model. Unfortunately, I was an anomaly and undoubtedly, for some, an annoying one. After all, our local church culture was based on male leadership. Most of my adult life I've been so immersed in church work I seldom stopped long enough to take a serious look at why it was so hard as a woman with a leadership gift to "serve well" without offending the men around me. I assumed there must be a good reason somewhere in Scripture besides my lack of people skills and male egos. Years later, I realize it was simply biased theology and the misrepresentation of Scripture regarding the roles of women.

It goes without saying that my own restlessness with the covert and overt depreciation of womanhood was magnified by my unsanctified nature. Admittedly, I resented the preferential treatment given to men in roles of leadership while chafing under the restricted roles prescribed to women. I also grew tired of dancing around some men's egos to ensure they didn't feel upstaged by a woman's abilities and gifts as a leader.

The Games We Play

At times it felt like the game we played as kids called "follow-the-leader," except in the church only "big boys" could lead whether they were qualified or not. I no longer want to play that game anymore than I want to play the "blame game." What I do want is to share my own story, which in turn will shed light on the detrimental, unbiblical mandates both men and women have bought into within hyper-conservative Christianity.

As you join us (Eric and Carol) on our journey of discovery, we hope you too will begin to ask the whys of gender roles and discrimination and find the conviction to promote change where it is needed. We hope to offer compelling reasons why believers and church leaders alike need to speak out against gender injustice and in support of women's equality. The Gospel invites women to join men in leading the way into the challenging future facing Christian ministry and marriage.

Part I

Rethinking Patriarchy in the Church

"Let the woman be satisfied with her state of subjection and not take it amiss that she is made inferior to the more distinguished sex." —**John Calvin**

"There is neither Jew nor Gentile, neither slave nor free, nor is there male and female, for you are all one in Christ Jesus." —**the Apostle Paul**

Chapter One

Christian Patriarchy, an Oxymoron?

The role of women in ministry and marriage is a highly debated topic among church leadership in many Christian denominations across the Protestant, Catholic, and Orthodox spectrums. Certainly within the conservative evangelical movement where Carol and I (Eric) spent much of our ministry. Much traditional Christian theology has declared the patriarchal position of male leadership and subsequent submission of women to be God's design and ideal for society, marriage, and the church.

In contrast to Christian patriarchy, Carol and I have come to believe in what is referred to as biblical egalitarianism. This is the theological belief that in creation and in Christ God endowed men and women with equal status, giving them the same rights and opportunities to serve in both the church and home based on their gifts. Biblical egalitarians believe the relationship of men and women is to be characterized by mutuality rather than hierarchy. Many Christians may not be aware of the sheer level of volatility surrounding this controversy of whether women are mandated by God to function in a subordinate role to men.

A Fight Breaks Out

When I was still a young pastor, I can admit I was out of touch with the depth of emotions surrounding this controversy. It was during a luncheon with other pastors that my naiveté was exposed. For many years, I'd been the primary facilitator for a monthly ministerial meeting over lunch in my community. Instead of discussing local issues, I preferred to spice things up by introducing controversial cultural and theological topics like abortion, civil disobedience, homosexuality, or capital punishment. Fun, fun, fun!

The ordination of practicing homosexuals as ministers was one of the first topics we tackled. Interest ran high and was one of the best-attended luncheons. I asked a local Methodist pastor who supported said ordination to make his presentation to the other pastors in attendance. While intense, the meeting was congenial with each pastor challenging the speaker's position in one way or another.

For the prior mentioned luncheon, I had asked the Episcopalian rector to present his denomination's position in favor of the ordination of women in ministry. I always anticipated some tension related to differences surrounding various moral and theological subjects, but I never realized how provocative a topic the role of women could be. To avoid identifying with just one point of view, I brought a position paper from Western Seminary that presented various positions held by Christians on women in ministry.

I had expected a lively but rational and illuminating discussion, but I quickly realized I'd gravely underestimated the depth of passion and conviction each minister felt regarding this subject. The Episcopalian rector had spoken for only a few minutes when the fireworks began. The Conservative Baptist pastor interrupted him with a full biblical assault in opposition to the Episcopalian position. The pastor of the Foursquare Church, a denomination started by a woman, jumped in defensively to support women's ordination.

I found myself completely unprepared to facilitate what had become a less than civil debate. I ended the meeting as diplomatically as I could, distributing my impartial position paper as an "olive branch" to those who'd attended. Afterwards, I called the various ministers to apologize for my lack of foresight regarding the topic's explosive nature. In all my years of ministry before or after that event, no topic has evoked such intense emotions among my fellow ministers. It was one of those experiences you file in your ministerial "playbook" and do whatever you can to avoid. It also served as a warning to let sleeping dogs lie within my own congregation.

While I'd taken a soft traditional position that only restricted women from church eldership and key pastoral roles, even this was not without some controversy. For one, my wife had a clear gift of leadership that challenged my theology. After Carol and I left our full-time ministry positions, we both felt compelled to re-examine what the Bible has to say about women's roles in ministry and marriage. Our discoveries have been no less than revolutionary, changing our perspective dramatically. I now oppose what I consider to be injustice and unbiblical gender inequality and want to do everything in my power to promote the calling of women to partner with men in roles of leadership.

One major change I would make if given the chance to start my ministry over again would be to intentionally train and support both men and women in positions of leadership. I can think of a dozen women whose gifts would have greatly benefited our church if they'd been encouraged to pursue leadership. I feel an apology is in order for my own prejudice and failure as a pastor to equip them in accordance to the listing of spiritual gifts and calling in Ephesians 4:11-12. Given a chance to speak into the lives of younger pastors, I would unapologetically and dogmatically share my conclusions after fifty years of active ministry regarding women's roles. That is what this book represents for me.

Exposing Secular Patriarchy for What It Is

Throughout the world, patriarchy is a social system of domination and subjugation that establishes men as the authority over their households and religious activities. Like a cancer cell, it has so metastasized since sin first entered the world that it permeates the very fabric of human nature. Patriarchy is responsible for the incomprehensible suffering of millions of women and children throughout history. It can only be explained as diabolical and demonic and must be opposed. There is no place in the Christian community, whether in the church or home, where it should be welcomed. The battle lines must be clearly drawn between this worldly system and God's redemptive plan for the relationship between men and women.

According to the United Nations website, it is estimated that:

- Thirty-five per cent of women worldwide have experienced either physical and/or sexual violence at some point in their lives.

- Of eighty-seven thousand women intentionally killed globally in 2017, more than half (fifty thousand, or fifty-eight per cent) were killed by intimate partners or family members, meaning that every day one hundred-thirty-seven women across the world are killed by a member of their own family. More than a third (thirty thousand) of women intentionally killed in 2017 were killed by their current or former intimate partner.

- Women and girls together account for seventy-one per cent of all human trafficking victims globally. Nearly three out of every four trafficked women and girls were for the purpose of sexual exploitation. At least three million women and girls are currently enslaved in the sex trade.

- Six hundred and fifty million women and girls in the world today were married before age eighteen. Child marriage often results in early pregnancy, social isolation, and interruption in schooling, which in turn limits a girl's opportunities and increases her risk of experiencing domestic violence.

- At least two hundred million women and girls alive today in the thirty countries with available data have undergone female genital mutilation. In most of these countries, the majority of girls were cut before age five. With migration from these countries, female genital mutilation is becoming a practice with global dimensions, in particular among refugee women and girls.

- Approximately fifteen million adolescent girls (aged fifteen to nineteen) worldwide have experienced forced sex (forced sexual intercourse or other sexual acts) at some point in their life. Out of these, nine million adolescent girls were victimized within the past year.

- In many countries, adolescent girls are most at risk of forced sex by a current/former husband, partner, or boyfriend. Based on data from thirty countries, only one percent ever seek professional help.

- Worldwide, women ages fifteen to forty-four are more likely to be maimed or die from male violence than from cancer, malaria, traffic accidents, and war combined.

- Every nine seconds, a woman in the United States is assaulted or beaten.

- Around the world, at least one in every three women has been beaten, coerced into sex, or otherwise abused during her lifetime.

When you get to the bottom of almost every injustice worldwide, you will find the inequality and oppression of women as a root cause. Study after study shows that societies characterized by the subjugation of women are more violent, corrupt, and impecunious than societies that empower women. It is a proven fact that empowering women decreases abuse, increases economic productivity, reduces infant mortality, contributes to overall improved health and nutrition, and increases the opportunities of education for the next generation.

THE CHURCH IS NOT IMMUNE

The average person is likely somewhat aware of how women suffer throughout the world under the domination of men. But they may be less aware of the severe inequality between men and women even found in the global church. Our years of involvement in global missions has made us disturbingly aware of the harmful result of patriarchy within the culture of many developing countries as well as the Christian community.

Shortly after our retirement from the pastorate, I (Carol) spent four months in a developing nation teaching on leadership and church management. Due to the danger as a foreign national of kidnapping or other assault, I spent those months surrounded 24/7 by armed guards. But nothing could protect me from the sorrow mixed with outrage I felt when confronted with the injustice of the Christian subculture.

Although this wasn't my first trip to this country, while teaching at the seminary I had a greater opportunity to connect with women who shared their heartbreaking stories as victims of cruelty and abuse. I became acutely aware that much of the way women were abused and devalued in this culture was a result of an already existing patriarchal social system finding the support of Christian theology within the church. Women were under their husband's control and regarded as property. A total dependence of women on their husbands gave them few rights and even less protection from domestic abuse.

Women shared with me how their husbands would deny them and their children food as a form of control and punishment. Husbands were permitted to beat their wives when displeased with them. One missionary shared with me that during one pastor's conference she attended a topic for discussion was how severe a beating was permissible for a good Christian husband.

Women also bear the burden of giving her husband many children, preferably boys. Meanwhile, all custody rights to the children belonged to the man. During this trip, I observed a baby dedication not unlike many others I had enjoyed. There was the expected exuberance as a processional of family members came down the center aisle, followed by an uncooperative goat that served as a thanksgiving offering. The father bringing his child to be dedicated had been childless for years so there was a heightened sense of celebration.

But after the service, I discovered something that left me with a sickening feeling. The joyful father had sent his previous wife back to her parents after many years of her not conceiving children. He'd then married a younger woman who was able to give him the son he wanted. This situation highlights how easy it is to justify injustice when inequality between men and women is accepted even within the church. When men are esteemed as more important than women, abuse and discrimination becomes justifiable.

It is to be expected that distinct characteristics and traditions of different indigenous cultures find expression in the church. The problem is when these cultural values and traditions violate principles taught in the Bible, including the liberty and equality for women. Obviously, many developing nations have difficult battles to fight with lack of education and employment opportunities, limited access to food, and other needs putting women at greater risk than the population as a whole. Scarcity always creates a distinct survival of the fittest, and women, being lower on the food chain, are severely handicapped and easily neglected.

But regardless of cultural circumstances, the church is accountable to more accurately represent Kingdom culture on earth. Jesus taught us to pray for his Kingdom to be expressed on earth as it is in heaven (Matthew 6:10). In his teaching, he contrasts the radical difference between worldly culture and Kingdom culture.

> But Jesus called them together and said, "You know that the rulers in this world lord it over their people, and officials flaunt their authority over those under them. But among you it will be

different. Whoever wants to be a leader among you must be your servant, and whoever wants to be first among you must become your slave. For even the Son of Man came not to be served but to serve others and to give his life as a ransom for many." (Matthew 20:25; cf. Luke 22:25, Mark 10:42.)

This radical teaching and its ramifications to relationships is inseparable to the gospel. Yet many churches are not only failing to protect women but promote teachings and beliefs that expose women to oppression and abuse. Frequently when sharing here in the United States of how women suffer in developing countries, my listeners seem impassive. Maybe because the problem seems so far removed from where they live it's hard to imagine there is really anything to be done. But is that really the case?

Chapter Two

Closer to Home

While in western nations and cultures, we no longer typically accept overt practices of discrimination against women, there is substantial evidence that the traditional teaching of patriarchy has negative effects in both church and home. Studies reveal that spousal abuse is just as common within the church as anywhere else. This means about twenty-five percent of Christian homes witness abuse of some kind.

Denise George, a gifted writer and wife of theologian Timothy George, published a book called *What Women Wish Pastors Knew*. She writes:

> Spouse abuse shocks us. We just cannot believe that a church deacon or member goes home after worship . . . and beats his wife.

Astonishingly, George notes that some of these men justify their violence by citing biblical passages. It is truly a sad reality that the Bible should be used to sanction abuse. In an article titled "Silent No More: Exposing Abuse Among Evangelicals," the author states:

I've heard stories from women who have struggled with their faith in God because they were abused by men. These women were emotionally, physically, sexually, and spiritually abused by husbands, fathers, uncles, brothers, pastors, or other men close to home. Their abusers believe that Scripture (and therefore God) gives men authority to monitor, manage, and discipline women. Longing to please God, these women submitted to abusive men, regardless of the cost to themselves. Some nearly lost their lives; others went into hiding. All are deeply wounded.

Such stories are not few and far between. For the past thirty years, Christians for Biblical Equality (CBE) has provided resources that challenge the idea of male authority as a biblical mandate. They have walked alongside women suffering from the abuse of men because of the imbalance of power and authority supported by patriarchy. There is clear evidence that without mutuality and equality, the relationship between a husband and wife is more susceptible to becoming abusive.

Examples of this are powerfully documented in Ruth Tucker's book *Black and White Bible, Black and Blue Wife*, which recounts her own abusive marriage and the theology that fueled her husband's violence. Tucker is a prolific scholar and highly regarded historian who has brought to light countless examples of women's influence as leaders in church history. In her work, she establishes women's capacity for leadership and challenges churches and denominations to liberate women and welcome their gifts. Even with these accomplishments, Ruth was abused in her own marriage by a man who used Scripture to oppress her. You may wonder as we did how this was even possible. How could a woman with her position and education have been so vulnerable?

That is, in fact, the insidious nature of the abuse of spiritual authority. There is a well-documented cycle of shame and guilt associated with abuse that keeps the victim silent and subjected while the perpetrator persists. While it may seem hard to understand how perpetrators get away with abuse, when you consider the message received by boys and girls that males have authority over women, there is no mystery. I know from my (Carol) own experience how this intimidation works.

Victims Remain Silent

I remember vividly when this first happened to me as a young girl. While at a park with my family, I was headed to the public swimming pool when a group of boys approached me. They coaxed me into following them by claiming they had something special to show me. Leading me into a thick hedge, they formed a circle around me, pushed me to the ground, then pulled out knives and demanded that I take off my clothes. In a state of shock, I felt initially paralyzed and unable to move.

What happened next can only be explained as a supernatural intervention that must have startled them as much as it did me. All I can remember is starting to unbuckle my belt while lying on the ground. The next thing I knew, I was standing on my feet. Not even considering how outnumbered I was, I managed to break through the circle without much resistance. While I can hardly remember the details of how I escaped, I do remember the feeling of relief once back to the safety of my parents.

As equally inexplicable as my escape was that I acted as though nothing had happened. My parents had no idea what had just happened to me, and I wasn't going to tell them. When I left the park with my parents later that day, this same gang of boys blatantly paraded by me. I still remember their mocking stares as they assumed a posture of dominant power, somehow knowing that I hadn't and wouldn't say a word.

So why did I remain silent? What happened to my voice? I had just been assaulted by a gang of boys at knife point. Why did I keep such a trauma to myself? What other young girls were victimized that same day? How would things have been different if I'd spoken up? Even in retelling this story, I feel a sense of shame as though it was my fault. Shouldn't I have known better than to follow those boys just because they asked?

I recall my mom sharing a story from her childhood about a neighbor who would sit her on his lap and touch her private parts. When she mentioned this to her mother, she was just told not to go over to his house. That was it!

It was as though this kind of behavior was to be expected from men, and it was a girl's responsibility to avoid those situations, so if it happened, it was somehow your own fault. One thing I know is that where male dominance and superiority is communicated in any way, a victim mentality can take root in the hearts of our girls while boys can become abusers.

DEEMED INFERIOR

All women are born into a world where they will face the unwelcome reality of their disadvantaged status based solely on gender. This awareness perpetuates a victim mindset in many women, resulting in a feeling of helplessness or powerlessness. In her book *From Bondage to Bonding,* Nancy Groom writes:

> Self-contempt is an expression of the belief that one's personhood is hopelessly flawed and unchangeable. Nothing speaks to one's personhood more than gender. If one's gender has been deemed inferior or second rate, there will be negative ramifications.

A study conducted by Baylor University revealed that violence is more likely to occur in homes where the husband has the power and makes all the decisions than in a home where there is shared leadership and joint decision-making. Another study from the University of Minnesota shows that traditional patriarchal couples experience spousal abuse at a rate more than four times higher than in marriages where mutuality is practiced. This affirms what has been acknowledged by many family therapy professionals. While patriarchal theology doesn't necessarily advocate abuse, its authority structure and imbalance of power coupled with sinful human nature invites trouble. Such an arrangement violates everything we know about healthy relationships.

To make matters worse, churches don't do enough to ensure the protection of women who are abused in relationships of female subordination. Pastors have been known to do more harm than good, assuming reports of abuse to be false or exaggerated. Nor have they thought enough about the gray area between "submission" and "abuse." If this sounds like we're being too hard on pastors, here are the astonishing results of a survey in which some six thousand pastors were asked how they would counsel a woman who came to them for help with domestic violence.

- Twenty-six percent responded that they would counsel the wife to continue submitting to her husband, no matter what.

- Twenty-five percent said they'd advise the wife that the abuse was partially her own fault for failing to submit in the first place.

- Fifty percent said that the wife should be willing to "tolerate some level of violence" because that was better than divorce.

The above counsel given to abused women is often the direct result of the teaching of Christian patriarchy!

A Surprise Change of Heart

Recently, in what was to me (Eric) a laudable but shocking reversal of personal conviction, Dr. Wayne Grudem, one of the foremost leaders of the Christian patriarchy movement in the United States, changed his long-standing theological position of permitting divorce for only two reasons: infidelity and desertion. Based on 1 Corinthians 7:15, he now believes that the Scriptures would allow for divorce as a result of abuse in the following areas.

- Extreme, prolonged, verbal and relational cruelty that is destroying the spouse's mental and emotional stability.

- Credible threats of physical harm or murder of spouse or children.

- Incorrigible (or recalcitrant, or inveterate, or incurable) drug or alcohol addiction accompanied by regular lies, deceptions, thefts, and/or violence.

- Incorrigible gambling addiction that has led to massive, overwhelming indebtedness.

- Pornography addiction would also fit here, but it would also be included under meaning of "sexual immorality" (Gk. *porneia*) in Matthew 19:9.

Although Dr. Grudem supports this new viewpoint biblically, at least part of his change of heart appears to have come from the personal stories of people who were trapped in abusive marriages. In a recent article in *Christianity Today* (November 2019) entitled, "Wayne Grudem Changes Mind about Divorce in Cases of Abuse," Dr. Grudem stated:

> My wife, Margaret, and I became aware of some heartbreaking examples of such things as severe sexual humiliation and degradation that had continued for decades, and another case of physical battering that had gone on for decades. In all these situations the abused spouse had kept silent, believing that a Christian's duty was to preserve the marriage unless there was adultery or desertion which had not happened.

Dr. Grudem, in telling the story of a woman who had remained silent for years in an abusive relationship believing this was what God expected of a Christian wife, added:

> That was just the most recent of a number of other cases where based on my theological instinct, I just can't see that this is the way God wants his children to live.

I cannot overstate my esteem for Dr. Grudem and how his sense of compassion and kindness motivated him to take another look at his scriptural understanding of divorce. However, I don't understand why his same "theological instincts" have not motivated him to also re-evaluate his scriptural understanding of Christian patriarchy and renounce the theological position that requires women to be subordinate to men, making them vulnerable to abuse. This teaching is also responsible for many "heartbreaking examples of such things as severe sexual humiliation and degradation." In applying Dr. Grudem's logic to the abuse found in Christian patriarchy, I am in complete agreement with him when he states, "I just can't see that this is the way God wants his children to live."

No Surprise At All!

According to another recent article in *Christianity Today* (May 2019) entitled "Ten Women Who Are Changing the Southern Baptist Response to Abuse," the evangelical church hasn't had eyes to see or ears to hear the extent of its own abuse crisis. Speaking to the problem of abuse in Christian marriages and the church, Beth Moore, a renowned Bible teacher, is quoted as saying:

By and large, the naïve couldn't fathom it, the knowledgeable wouldn't risk it, the perpetrators were good at it, and the victims were shamed and blamed for it.

If there are even remnants of misogyny and discrimination rooted in one's view of womanhood, the lines between submission and abuse are blurred and the sound of women's voices is muffled. Leaders are simply not connecting the dots to how this theology misrepresents Kingdom values and the equality of women, not only in developing countries, but in our own backyard. Many church leaders have closed their eyes to how the patriarchal theology promoted in conservative evangelical churches diminish the gospel message.

We may not be able to eliminate all oppression of women worldwide. But we can have greater influence in promoting the unobstructed gospel message representing both men and women in the church. Whether or not the church in North America wants to take responsibility for what is happening in the church worldwide, many in other nations look to us as an example. Much Christian theology is exported from North America to churches around the world, giving us a serious charge to take a second look at what we are sending abroad.

The church can and should take a stronger stand to expose abuse instead of exposing women to abuse. J.D. Greear, president of the Southern Baptist Convention, states that we need to "repent of a culture that has made abuse, cover-ups, and evading accountability far too easy." One strategic step forward in that process of repentance would be for church leaders to reexamine their theological position regarding womanhood and manhood. If we don't get this foundational issue right, then everything will remain skewed, and the gospel message will always be tainted by granting more power to men than women.

Kudos to the many churches who are rallying against the unthinkable degradation of sex trafficking. We believe this is a cause that desperately needs our support. We have seen this need in developing nations especially and have supported the training of at-risk women to become seamstresses, nurses, and micro-business owners. Without marketable skills, prostitution remains for many women one of the most viable options for survival. It goes without saying the church should support the liberation of women from sex trafficking. But when it comes to the more subtle depreciation and abuse of women in the church and home, we can miss the forest for the trees.

BENEVOLENT PATRIARCHY?

Studies indicate that just exhorting men to treat women better isn't going to solve the problem. Anytime and anywhere a gender or race is given greater power over others, the seeds of disregard, disrespect, and abuse will more readily germinate. Marg Mowczko, a prolific blogger, in her article, *Is a Benevolent Patriarchy Good for God's People?* writes:

> Apartheid, even if enacted with benevolence and kindness, is a social system where one group of people is more, and another group is less. Slavery, even when the master is benevolent and

kind, is a social system where the master is more, and the slaves are less.

Patriarchy, or a traditional understanding of male "headship," even when the man is benevolent and kind, is a social system where man is more, and woman is less. In these three systems, the people belonging to one group have more power, prestige, and social freedoms than those in the other group.

It is far too easy to overlook how patriarchy promotes an insidious deviation from Kingdom values such as mutual submission and servanthood. As Christians, we can be culture-shapers by modeling a radically different value system.

Whether you call patriarchy biblical or Christian or simply give it some other nicer-sounding name, it is still patriarchy. Because of the obvious negative images associated with a straight-up, in-your-face definition of patriarchy, leaders in the Christian community have come up with a "kinder, gentler" word known as *complementarianism*. While this term sounds more sensitive and caring than the associations to male dominance that patriarchy carries, the harmful outcomes of this theological system are the same.

With the adoption of the word complementarian, it can be difficult to determine what exactly is the position being taken by each church. Views of hierarchal gender roles range on a continuum from hardline patriarchy where men hold all the power to a softer approach where women are primarily excluded from senior pastor/elder roles. Our observation is that the term complementarian serves as an ambiguous label that provides opponents of biblical egalitarianism with a very broad rallying point for their collective opposition.

When you look at what complementarians are advocating, it becomes clear the verbiage in their position is only modified ever so slightly. They state upfront that men and women are of equal value in their personhood. That said, men and women have different and "complementary" roles and responsibilities in marriage, family life, religious leadership, and elsewhere.

Initially this all sounds reasonable until the smoke clears and a closer examination makes clear that complementarianism still means men are to rule over women while women are to submit to men. All you need to do is read the first chapter of the complementarian's magnum opus *Recovering Biblical Manhood and Womanhood* to see how their advocacy for female subordination plays out between all men and all women in all situations. Whether in the workplace or in worship, in the church or in the home, men are meant to lead women and women are invited to respond by supporting their leadership.

In summary, complementarianism is simply a euphemism for Christian patriarchy. It is an attempt to substitute a positive, less offensive term for a concept that is rightfully perceived to be domineering and a misrepresentation of fundamental principles of the Kingdom of God. When it comes to marriage, no matter how much the church discusses the servanthood role of male leadership and the willing submission of women, the imbalance of power at best results in benevolent sexism. Christian patriarchy, or complementarianism, defines masculinity and femininity primarily in terms of leadership and submission: leadership as an intrinsically masculine quality while the fundamental role of women is to be submissive and responsive to male leadership in the church and home.

In the end, we are suggesting that the real struggle is not between biblical egalitarianism and complementarianism or between non-traditional and traditional roles for men and women, but between true biblical equality and inequality. The inequality of patriarchy not only opens the door to abuse and even misogyny but shuts the door to gifts and abilities desperately needed by the church. As the social climate is heating up with countless women speaking out to expose the degrading and abusive behavior of men in positions of authority, the issue of male dominance in the church is gaining attention.

Proverbial Applecart

This clamoring in our secular culture is reverberating in the church and upsetting the proverbial applecart. Church leaders appear quite concerned about how far the apples are going to roll regarding the traditional functions and responsibilities of Christian men and women. As believers, we need to be prepared to address radical elements of the secular feminist movement that want to eliminate all gender distinctions. But how can we possibly speak against the extremes of this movement in a relevant, compassionate, and informed way while the church supports male privilege and women are not acknowledged as equal representatives of the image of God? If we want to be taken seriously by our culture, we need to be willing to take a second look at what the church is communicating to emerging generations about the role of women. We must ask the question whether we are truly communicating what God's Word is on this matter.

Sadly, some influential Christian leaders are becoming even more adamant in their support of patriarchy and their opposition to egalitarianism. They insist that any deviation from a masculine leadership model is a direct challenge to God's Word and erodes the essence of the gospel. At the same time, we are seeing numerous pastors who once supported the hierarchical view wrestling more honestly with the very scriptures that have been used to oppose women in ministry. Others have embraced shared leadership, accepting both qualified men and women as pastors and elders.

The average church member has by default bought into the traditional position that denies women roles in leadership. They are often in the dark about what is at stake in this debate and the severity of the ramifications as to how the church responds. We (Carol and Eric) were certainly in the dark throughout much of our ministry. Our hope is that we can turn the light on to expose patriarchy as a deviation from God's original design for the male-female relationship. We encourage men and women to gain a better understanding of what the Bible teaches, and history affirms about God's ultimate plan for his image-bearers.

Chapter Three

The Very Best Scenario

It is exciting to see the ground swell of sincere believers asking questions about women's roles and feeling dissatisfaction with traditional answers. One overarching question in particular drives this debate. Is there a divine order to the subordination of women that gives men the dominant role in ministry and marriage, or does God call and gift women to take leadership roles in mutual partnerships with men? In our research, we discovered that history and Scripture give very different answers to this question.

Of course, what God has to say needs to be the final court of appeal, and each side of the debate believes they have Scripture to support their conviction. Ultimately, it is the responsibility of every Christian to ask this crucial question and find a biblical answer. Starting at the beginning in Genesis and tracking God's epic story all the way through Revelation, we believe Scripture provides biblical support for mutuality and partnership as God's original intention for the relationship of men and women.

Let's begin with the creation story of man and woman since this is central to understanding God's original design for their intended purpose and partnership. The creation of mankind was unlike any of God's other creative acts. After each day of creation, we see God taking pleasure in his finished work: "And God saw that it was good" (Genesis 1:4, 10, 12, 18, 25).

But on the sixth and final day, something different happens. Immediately following the creation of mankind, we hear God saying, "It is not good" (Genesis 2:18). But by the end of the day, there is another climactic announcement: "And God saw that it was *very* good" (Genesis 1:31). To get the picture God intends us to see here, we need to synchronize the two creation accounts of mankind found in the first two chapters of Genesis. So much rests on a correct understanding of the unique creative progression of God as he fashions his image-bearers, man and woman. Let's look at the first account in chapter one.

> Then God said, "Let us make mankind in our image, in our likeness, so that they may rule over the fish in the sea and the birds in the sky, over the livestock and all the wild animals, and over all the creatures that move along the ground." So God created mankind in his own image, in the image of God he created them; male and female he created them. God blessed them and said to them, "Be fruitful and increase in number; fill the earth and subdue it. Rule over the fish in the sea and the birds in the sky and over every living creature that moves on the ground. Then God said, "I give you every seed-bearing plant on the face of the whole earth and every tree that has fruit with seed in it. They will be yours for food. And to all the beasts of the earth and

all the birds in the sky and all the creatures that move along the ground—everything that has the breath of life in it—I give every green plant for food." And it was so. God saw all that he had made, and it was very good. And there was evening, and there was morning—the sixth day. (Genesis 1:26-28)

We can make several precedent-setting observations from this creation narrative. First, God refers to himself as a plural "us." This is significant because God as a plural "us" is proposing to create mankind to reflect his likeness. In fact, to be God's image bearer will require an "us." God exists as a triune God in a union of Personhood. So God creates mankind as male and female. Both are created in God's image. Both are blessed and commissioned to rule over all that God created. Both are instructed on how food will be provided for them and for "everything that has the breath of life in it" (vs. 26). Neither man nor woman is given individual role assignments suggesting a system of hierarchy. This creation narrative is clear and straightforward. It concludes with God now affirming that "it was very good."

Taking a Second Look

Now let's look at the second account of the sixth and final day of creation given in Genesis chapter two. Here is where some have erroneously read into certain ambiguities, giving rise to incorrect theology about the relationship between the man and the woman. Specifically, a supposed divine mandate of male leadership and female subordination based on a creation order. We can concede this may be easy to do if one comes to the text predisposed to a hierarchical mindset, which is humanity's historic natural default since the Fall, as we will see in Genesis chapter three.

> Then the LORD God formed a man from the dust of the ground and breathed into his nostrils the breath of life, and the man became a living being. Now the LORD God had planted a garden in the east, in Eden; and there he put the man he had formed . . .
>
> The LORD God took the man and put him in the Garden of Eden to work it and take care of it. And the LORD God commanded the man, "You are free to eat from any tree in the garden; but you must not eat from the tree of the knowledge of good and evil, for when you eat from it you will certainly die."
>
> The LORD God said, "It is not good for the man to be alone. I will make a helper suitable for him (a companion who corresponds to him)." Now the LORD God had formed out of the ground all the wild animals and all the birds in the sky. He brought them to the man to see what he would name them; and whatever the man called each living creature, that was its name. So the man gave names to all the livestock, the birds in the sky and all the wild animals. But for Adam no suitable helper (companion who corresponds to him) was found.
>
> So the LORD God caused the man to fall into a deep sleep; and while he was sleeping, he took one of the man's ribs (part of the man's side) and then closed up the place with flesh. Then the LORD God made a woman from the rib (part of the man's side) he had taken out of the man, and he brought her to the man. The man said, "This is now bone of my bones and flesh of my flesh; she shall be called 'woman,' *for she was taken out of man* (italics

added)." That is why a man leaves his father and mother and is united to his wife, and they become one flesh. (Genesis 2:7-24)

In this second creation narrative, we see a part of the creative progression not revealed in the first account. We are told that the woman was taken out of Adam, which is the Hebrew word meaning "mankind." The first creation account states that God created mankind, then goes on to amplify, "male and female created he them" (Genesis 1:26). It can be understood that Adam (mankind) as depicted in the second creation narrative represented both male and female in his personhood (as was indeed literally the case in his DNA).

God places Adam in the Garden and assigns him the task of naming the animals, all of whom had partners (companions corresponding to them) that were both male and female. Adam would have observed that in all God had created and pronounced "good" there was complementary completeness. The light and the darkness. The sun and the moon. The sky and the land. The sea and dry ground. Adam's own aloneness was profoundly obvious and incongruent with all that he saw in God's creation.

Here is where we read for the first time God stating that something isn't good. Specifically, God declares that man's aloneness, his lack of a counterpart, is not good. It was the only part of creation deemed unacceptable and incomplete. This initiates the unique, one-of-a-kind creation of the woman. Up to this point "all thing that have the breath of life," including mankind, were formed from the dust (Genesis 1:30). But the woman is "taken out of the man" and fashioned by God as a complementary image bearer. At the end of the sixth day, after creating the man and the woman, God makes his final pronouncement: "It was very good" (Genesis 1:31).

ADAM, MALE AND FEMALE

In Genesis 1:26-28 and 5:1-2, we are told that God's image is expressed in both male and female human beings rather than in just one male. In fact, it is reasonable to understand that Adam as he was formed from the dust (chapter 2) was both male and female in personhood until woman was "taken out" of Adam. We read that God put Adam into a deep sleep and performed surgery on him. God took something out of him. Traditionally, this something is referred to as a rib. But in the text, it can refer to a "part" of his side. Part of Adam was integral to the creation of the first woman.

When Adam woke from his deep sleep, something of his essence was missing. When he saw the woman for the first time, he made several statements indicating this. One was "she was taken out of man!" The progressive narrative of the creation of man and woman depicts the initiation of a unique relationship of mutuality and intimacy orchestrated by God. God introducing the woman to the man is a beautiful depiction of the first marriage ceremony. It is like the father of the bride walking his daughter down the aisle to present her to the groom.

When Adam first lays eyes on his bride, he exclaims, "This one at last is bone of my bone and flesh of my flesh," another profound expression of oneness. To further emphasize the point, verse 24 says that when a husband and wife join in marriage, they become "one flesh." The creation account of Eve is brief and enigmatic, but its purpose is surely to illustrate the equality, affinity, and unity of the first man and woman and their joint purpose of caring for the earth.

SOMEONE'S MISSING

We might ask why God created mankind, Adam, as just one human only to announce that this aloneness wasn't good, then go on to create two humans out of the one. Was this a teaching moment for mankind to understand their incompleteness without a counterpart?

We can't fully know God's intention, but it does seem a brilliant way to introduce the symbiotic relationship God intended for the man and the woman and to stage the very first marriage. In this scene where the woman is presented to the man, we see one of the first expressions of God's personal love for his children and his desire for relationship. Adam first experiences unwelcome aloneness, then is given someone with whom to share mutual love and companionship.

A severe misrepresentation has been made in attempting to explain why and how the woman was created. Here is where complementarian Christian leaders try to substantiate their patriarchal theology. One such conjecture is to project roles and hierarchy into the very beginning of the relationship between the man and the woman. We hope to show how this undermines God's original design and misrepresents the very nature of God.

Clearly, the attempt to attribute the man with God-given authority and responsibility over the woman based on creation order is without warrant. Especially when you consider that the animals were created before mankind. That may sound silly but makes about as much sense as referring to Adam as the woman's superior because he was formed first. And like all the animals but unlike the woman, Adam was formed from the dust. What does that make Adam? Less than the woman? More like the animals? Just imagine what kind of theological nonsense could be drawn by making assumptions from such details.

The assignment Adam was given to name the animals (Genesis 2:19, 20) is also conjectured to suggest his primacy over the woman when in fact both the man and the woman were given authority to rule over the animals (Genesis 1:28). Using that reasoning would be like suggesting man's inferiority based on his job description as just the gardener and zookeeper until the woman came on the scene (Genesis 2:15). It is after she is created that God gave them both the assignment to rule over the created world.

On a more serious note, a topic germane to the controversy about women's roles in relationship to men centers on the meaning of the word *'ēzer kĕnegĕdô*, or helpmate, often interpreted to relegate women to serve men as a helper. The structure of the creation narrative climaxes in the creation of woman, fulfilling man's need for a partner corresponding to him (Genesis 2:18, 20). The text describes man's recognition of his need for someone like him. "But for Adam no companion who corresponded to him was found" (Genesis 2:20). The verbiage implies Adam was looking for that someone as he named the animals but couldn't find who he was looking for.

DIVINE PARTNERSHIP

The LORD God said, "It is not good for the man to be alone. I will make a companion for him who corresponds to him" (Genesis 2:18). The Hebrew word used here is ʽēzer kĕnegĕdô, literally "a strength corresponding to him." Unfortunately, the word ʽēzer here is often translated "helper" or "helpmeet," which in English implies a subordinate, servant, or someone inferior in skill and ability. So we look at this phrase and assume the woman was made to be an assistant to the man.

Here's the big surprise. Never in the Bible does ʽēzer suggest "helper" as implying a servant or assistant. In fact, the word ʽēzer is almost always used to describe God as his people's savior, rescuer, strength, or might (Exodus 18:4, Deuteronomy 33:7, 26, 29, Psalm 20:2; 33:20; 70:5; 89:19; 115:9, 10, 11; 121:1, 2; 124:8; 146:5, Hosea 13:9). One of the most authoritative biblical Hebrew dictionaries, *The Hebrew and Aramaic Lexicon of the Old Testament* by Koehler, Walter and Stamm, lists biblical meanings of ʽēzer as "help, assistance, might, and strength," much like the above-mentioned descriptions of God. It is never listed as "helper" or "assistant." Additionally, we find that ʽēzer is used three times to describe a military protector (Isaiah 30:5, Ezekiel 12:14, Daniel 11:34). Nothing in the context of any of these passages warrants concluding that as ʽēzer woman must be subordinate to man.

It is imperative to recognize that Adam was never appointed independently from the woman as the ruler of the world. Nor did he receive the commission to fill the earth and subdue it alone. God gave that command to both Adam and Eve in Genesis 1:28, where we read that "God blessed *them* and said to *them*, 'be fruitful and increase in number; fill the earth and subdue it.'"

Adam was incapable of fulfilling God's will on his own. The only way for him to fill the earth and subdue it was in partnership with "a strength corresponding to him." So God provided Eve as his partner, companion, and co-ruler. She was there by his side as they were given the power and authority to fulfill the task as co-regents who equally represented the image of God (Genesis 1:26–27).

What we must conclude is that the designation of the woman as *'ēzer kĕnegĕdô* (Genesis 2:18) challenges the concept of male headship and identifies the woman as one who comes to rescue man from being incomplete and alone. She is his counterpart, his companion and friend who joins him in exercising dominion over the earth. She completes or enables him so that together they can fulfill their God-given responsibilities.

What the second retelling of the creation story does establish is man's need for a companion suitable "to" him, not "for" him. That is, a partner to serve *with* him, not a helper to assist him. It isn't surprising that the apostle Paul's theology reflects this New Testament value of mutuality between men and women when he affirms the reality of man and woman's interdependency in his first epistle to the Corinthian church.

> In the Lord woman is not independent of man or man of woman; for as woman was made from man, so man is now born of woman. And all things are from God. (I Corinthians 11:11-12)

Chapter Four

But Isn't God Male?

Candidly speaking, my (Eric) greatest struggle in addressing the issue of women in ministry arose from my hesitation to accept the idea that God is revealed in the Bible as both male and female. How could that be possible?

What follows is the result of our cautious and careful inquiry into this concept. As I trudged forward in my study of the nature of God, Bruxy Cavey, pastor of The Meeting House in Ontario, Canada, provided significant insights along the way. A major breakthrough came when I recognized the obvious fact that God is first and foremost a spirit. In John 4:24, Jesus declared emphatically that "God is spirit." As spirit, God is not literally a gendered being even though he is revealed analogically to us in Scripture through gendered human language.

This line of thinking is also reflected in the warning Moses received from God himself not to make idols identifying God with any physical form nor to envision God as a super-man or super-woman.

> You saw no form of any kind (neither male nor female) the day the Lord spoke to you at Horeb out of the fire. Therefore, watch yourselves very carefully, so that you do not become corrupt and make for yourselves an idol, and image of any shape, whether formed like a man or a woman. (Deuteronomy 4:15-17)

Finally, it is important to note that God discloses his personal name to Moses when he says, "I AM who I AM" (Exodus 3:14). What may surprise you is that this name of God we commonly reference as Yahweh is neither a masculine nor feminine name but a genderless name. In describing himself as Yahweh, the I AM, God is simply pointing to the eternity of his existence, to his entity, to himself as the existence of life, the being of God.

In fact, if the nature of God was exclusively male in some ultimate metaphysical sense, we would expect the Trinity to be described as "Father, Son, and Older Brother," or "Father, Son, and Grandfather." Instead, God describes himself as "Father, Son, and Holy Spirit." In using "Spirit" as part of God's self-disclosure, he opens the door to the revelation that God also communicates qualities about himself which are decisively feminine. We know this for several reasons. First, in Greek the term Spirit (πνεῦμα, pneûma) is gender neutral. In Hebrew, the term Spirit (רוּחַ, rūaḥ) is feminine. Further, we note in John 14:26 that the Spirit is also called "the Comforter" (ὁ παράκλητος – ho parakletos), which in the Greek is masculine. The point here is simple. God the Holy Spirit is not limited or restricted to any specific human gender.

Numerous Christian creeds such as the Athanasius Creed have consistently declared that "the divinity of the Father, Son, and Holy

Spirit is one, their glory equal, their majesty co-eternal." The lack of a specific gender designation for the Spirit must be understood as a revelation of the very nature of God in which the male gender language used of the Father and the Son is excluded. Therefore, if we are made in the image of God, then God has revealed himself as both male and female. Accordingly, his Personhood is the ultimate source of the best of what it means to be male and the best of what it means to be female. As a result, the fullness of what it means to be human in our maleness and femaleness is found in the essence and nature of God as the source.

THE DUAL NATURE OF GOD

Unfortunately, this dual nature of God often goes unaddressed by Christian leaders, leaving the indelible impression on the minds of believers that God is exclusively masculine. Of course, this misconception flies in the face of biblical revelation, which in many places affirms just the opposite to be true. In the next section, Carol will share several passages that verify this truth.

So why do we see such a masculine lineup in Scripture? Obviously, the masculine aspect of God's nature is explicit since God repeatedly reveals himself as a father, not mother. As a father, he sent his eternal Son, not daughter, into the world as a man not as a woman. His Son then chose twelve male disciples to be his first apostles. God is seen as king, not queen, and so on. Doesn't this support the claim that God made Christianity and the church to have a masculine feel and a masculine ministry?

Such a claim may appear logical. But it completely ignores everything about the nature of God stated above as well as overlooking the historical and cultural context of these events. Theologians refer to this as culturally conditioned revelation in which God accommodates himself to the understanding of the people. If you are familiar with the narrative of the Fall, which we will cover in Genesis chapter three, men began to dominate women because of sin and the curse upon the world. Patriarchy became the worldwide social system under Satan's domain (Genesis 3:15). Consequently, let me lay out three reasons why we see the revelation of God as Father and men as the dominant leaders in the Bible.

THREE REASONS FOR THE FATHERHOOD OF GOD

First, as far as God revealing himself as the Father, we must note that within all ancient cultures, the father was considered the protector, provider, creator, progenitor, head of the family, and most importantly, the father-ruler. So for God to be revealed as Father in a fallen world is to use an appropriate cultural analogy identifying him as the head of our lives and of our families.

As such, it is appropriate to call him Father God. This communicates qualities about God that are important for us to understand. He is our leader, our protector, and our provider. He is a strong warrior and defender. These are traits that would never be communicated if referring to God as Mother, given the inferior role of women in the patriarchal social system. If God had said, "I'm really a mother god," that would have identified him as a secondary deity. Such a female deity would not be affirmed as the primary ruler of the universe. So God says, "I am your Father, but I will also teach you that I am a father who loves you like a mother."

Second, for the Son to come to earth in male form was also imperative if he ever hoped to have an audience and be taken seriously by a patriarchal culture. At that time and for most of human history, women had no voice, no education, and no opportunity to learn Torah or have a voice to speak with authority. So it is both understandable and practical that Jesus would come as a man and initially find it necessary to gather around himself twelve other male disciples. Considering that women were not allowed to lead, teach, or even speak to men, the only way the gospel message could initially be carried forward within that cultural context would be through men.

Thirdly, and perhaps a less obvious reason, Jesus came as the gender of power in order to teach his followers how to lay their power down. He came to teach men how to lay down their swords and pick up their crosses. He came to teach men how to humble themselves, get down on their knees, and wash one another's feet (John 13:1-17). He came to demonstrate how the greatest among them would be servant of all. He told the men he had chosen that he had come to teach them the way of meekness, the way of laying down power, the way of self-sacrifice and servanthood.

Think of it this way. If Jesus had come as a woman and said these things, his words would have fallen on deaf ears. Everyone would have said, "Of course you're telling us to do these things because that's what women do. That's your place. That's exactly what we want you to keep doing." The whole message of laying down your power would have made no sense coming from a gender that never had any power to begin with. Laying aside one's power only means something when you possess that power. This is what Jesus modeled as a man and teaches his male and female followers to do as well.

> Do nothing out of selfish ambition or vain conceit. Rather, in humility value others above yourselves, not looking to your own interests but each of you to the interests of the others. In your relationships with one another, have the same mindset as Christ Jesus Who, being in very nature God, did not consider equality with God something to be used to his own advantage; rather, he made himself nothing by taking the very nature of a servant, being made in human likeness. And being found in appearance as a man, he humbled himself by becoming obedient to death—even death on a cross! (Philippians 2:3-7)

Many people form images of God in their minds that if challenged cause confusion and alarm. The thought that God is both male and female is one of those images that may be quickly labeled as heretical. But the real heresy lies in teaching that God is only male and that which is feminine cannot be found in him. On the contrary, we will see in Scripture that as spirit God has both masculine and feminine characteristics.

The tradition of referring to God as solely masculine coupled with a lack of teaching about the dual masculine and feminine nature of God opens the door for many distortions, prejudices, and abuses to germinate. This can't help but contribute to the second-class status of women in the church. We need to break the conspiracy of silence about the feminine face of God that has contributed in some measure to the discrimination and disregard for women throughout the history of the church.

THE MOTHER HEART OF GOD

One of this universe's great mysteries is how God who is spirit chose to reveal himself as male and female. Together, masculinity and femininity reflect God in the material world. As image-bearers, the very first man and woman displayed God's goodness and glory to each other and all of creation. It was in choosing to reject God's design and intended purpose that this glorious image was lost. Finding it again is a significant part of what life's journey is about.

Growing up, I (Carol) remember depictions of God as an elderly man with white hair and a long white beard, a kind of heavenly Moses figure. Since God was always referred to with a masculine pronoun, I never thought to question that he could be anything other than male, much less to think of him in feminine terms. It wasn't until I went to Bible college that I was challenged to think more deeply about the nature of God.

As Eric already mentioned, John 4:24 tells us that God is spirit and therefore transcends gender. In this passage, which is the story of Jesus's encounter with the Samaritan woman at the well, we are invited to worship God in spirit and in truth. So our worship should be passionate and sincere (in spirit) as well as biblically accurate and informed (in truth). In my thinking, if we are to worship God biblically, accurately, and informed by the truth, it is imperative we are mindful that God imprinted both male and female with his image as a self-revelation of his nature (Genesis 1:24-25).

When Eric and I were attending Bible college together, we would playfully debate whether God was more male or female. At one point, we thought it would be fun to take our debate into the public arena. While planning an event for young married couples at the church where we ministered, we devised a humorous way to do just that. We staged a mock debate in which Eric posed as Reverend Pious Malarkey, advocating that God was solely male, while I as Sister Gabby Talk-a-Lot made a case for God being female.

I quoted Numbers 23:19, which states that "God is not a man that he should lie!" Tongue in cheek, I argued that since God couldn't lie, there was no way he could be a man. Eric used 1 Corinthians 14:34 in rebuttal, which says that women should remain silent in the churches for they are not permitted to speak but must be in submission. Pounding his fist on the pulpit, he emphasized how this confirmed that anything I had to say was irrelevant. In fact, I shouldn't be talking at all.

Our audience found our overstated caricatures hilarious with only a few ruffled feathers and bruised egos. At the time, we had no idea of the hostility brewing in the church between those defending the exclusivity of the masculine image of God and those advocating there were feminine characteristics to God's nature and personhood. Let's just say certain church fathers would have been turning in their graves at the thought of what I was postulating even humorously.

Avoiding Extremes

So here we are some forty years later addressing this topic again, except this time with a very serious objective in mind. We have undertaken this topic to help eliminate some prevailing thought memes that have ignored feminine imagery used to describe God. We have no plans to stop addressing God as Father or any of the other foolishness associated with extremes of the feminist movement. We are just unwilling to sit by while an opposite extreme is promoted without being challenged biblically.

In truth, Scripture is replete with examples of God's feminine characteristics as part of his self-revelation. There is overwhelming evidence that God reveals himself as both father and mother. Although for reasons Eric stated previously, God has primarily revealed himself in the role of father, God's essence and identity should not be viewed exclusively as male while ignoring his feminine characteristics.

Let's look together at just a few of the many places in Scripture where feminine images of God can be found. While less frequent than masculine images, they are none the less extremely significant. For example, God refers to himself in Genesis 17:1 as El Shaddai. El Shaddai is just one of many names of God in the Hebrew language. "El" means "God" while "shad" means "breast" in Hebrew. It is a powerful feminine image of God as a nursing mother with the breast being a key symbol of sustenance, protection, and parental love. In using this title, God is comparing himself to a mother while his people are depicted as his nursing children. This remarkable self-disclosure demonstrates God's commitment to nourish, satisfy, and supply for all the needs of his people as a mother would for her child.

The apostle Peter uses this same feminine breast-feeding imagery to instruct believers who have just been born again to crave the pure spiritual milk that God, like a nursing mother, is now offering them.

> Like newborn infants, longing for pure spiritual milk, that by it you may grow up into salvation. (1 Peter 2:2-3)

The Old Testament prophet Isaiah also uses such symbolic language in conveying God's loving call to his people.

> Listen to me, O house of Jacob, all the remnant of the house of Israel, who have been borne by me from before your birth, carried from the womb [some translations "from MY womb]. (Isaiah 46:3)

In commenting on this passage, the great Protestant scholar John Calvin commented:

> God has manifested himself to be both Father and Mother so that we might be more aware of God's constant presence and willingness to assist us. (Volume VII, Isaiah 33-77, page 436)

Later in Isaiah, God assures his people:

> Can a mother forget the baby at her breast and have no compassion on the child she has borne? Though she may forget, I will not forget you. (Isaiah 49:15)

Calvin goes on to comment on this verse:

> God did not satisfy himself with proposing the example of a father, but in order to express his very strong affection, he chose to liken himself to a mother, and calls his people not merely children, but the fruit of the womb, toward which there is usually a warmer affection.

Further, feminine images of God can be found in numerous passages. Yahweh asks Job, "From whose womb comes ice? Who gives birth to the frost from the heavens (Job 38:29)?" Isaiah speaks again of God being like "a woman in childbirth" (Isaiah 42:14). Jesus compares God to a woman seeking lost coins (Luke 15:8-10) and a mother hen gathering her chicks (Matthew 23:37). We could go on.

Each of these images signifies that God nurtures and protects as well as creates and redeems. Both the "power" language and "nurturing" language are equally reflective of God's character, just as male and female were both equally made in God's image to reflect the true character of God. What we see in Scripture is Father God with a mother's heart. In this we can hear God say, "I love like a father who chooses to be there for you in commitment and covenant, and I also love you like a mother who brought you into this world to love and nurture."

If we can grasp the true nature of God as both male and female and understand it in our minds and hearts, then we can begin to embrace and enjoy both the masculine and feminine care of God for his people.

Chapter Five

When Good Goes Very Bad

What happens in chapter three of Genesis is a reversal of everything God declares good and very good in the first two chapters. Words can't adequately describe the tragedy that unfolded when God's crown of creation unwittingly joins the satanic rebellion against God. God's world of beauty turns ugly and chaotic. The man and woman's relationship of mutuality and equality is lost to domination and control. Their rulership over the world is surrendered to Satan.

What happens when Adam and Eve succumb to Satan's temptation in the Garden of Eden explains why the world is in the condition it is. We can't underestimate how far mankind and the world have fallen from God's original design. To do so is to miss the severity of the impact on the relationship between men and women.

If you aren't familiar with this tragic drama, here is a summary of what goes very bad in the Garden. The backstory is that Satan leads a rebellion against God allied with one-third of the angels, which results in Satan and his followers being cast out of heaven (Revelation 12:4, 7-9, Luke 10:18, Isaiah 14:12-13). Satan's strategic retaliation is to take the form of a serpent and tempt the woman to disobey God's command not to eat of the Tree of the Knowledge of Good and Evil. Deceived into eating the forbidden fruit, the woman then offers it to the man, who also eats. Immediately, their eyes are opened to sin and evil, and they become aware that they are naked (Genesis 3:7).

In their rebellion, the man and woman lost their glory as God's image-bearers and experienced a death worse than dying, separation from their Life-giver and Source of all good things. This severing of their relationship with God began a cascading onslaught of consequences that would affect every part of the man and woman's lives as they found themselves overcome by feelings they'd never experienced before. Perfect love was replaced by fear. Contentment and peace were replaced by shame. Every man, woman, and child from that point forward would now experience this desolate state of separation from God, as the apostle Paul makes clear in his epistle to the church in Rome.

> For all have sinned and fall short of the glory of God. (Romans 3:23)

> For the wages of sin is death. (Romans 6:23a)

We can only imagine Adam and Eve's desperation to escape such overwhelming feelings of ear and shame. These are feelings we're all familiar with, but they'd never felt them before. If mood-altering substances had been available, they might have sought them out. Instead, not unlike many of us when confronted with our failures, they got busy. First on the list was to make clothes out of leaves to cover their nakedness. Judging by countless warm-weather cultures who have used such dress since, this was likely some sort of apron girdle that covered their intimate parts.

After getting dressed, Adam and Eve heard the once-welcome sound of God walking in the garden. Instead of being happy to see their Creator, the sound of his footsteps now magnifies their feelings of fear and shame, so they quickly hide. These foreign, frightening emotions would now be the new normal in their relationship with God and each other.

Hiding from God

God's first spoken words in redemptive history come in the form of a question (Genesis 3:9): "Where are you?" He doesn't need to be told where they are. In essence, he is asking, "Why are you hiding from me?"

While it is Adam who responds, his words reveal how both the man and woman's once-intimate relationship with God has now been replaced by self-protection and defensiveness. "I was afraid, so I hid" (Genesis 3:10). It is hard to imagine they ever thought they could hide from God. But who are we to judge? Been there, done that!

At some point, Adam and Eve were evidently convinced to step out of the bushes since we witness in their continued dialogue the further unraveling of their relationships with both God and each other. God asks his second probing question (Genesis 3:11): "Have you eaten from the tree whose fruit I commanded you not to eat?"

Adam responds by pointing his finger at the woman, indirectly blaming God as well as Eve. "It was the woman *you* gave me." When Eve is confronted, she joins the blame game and points her finger at the serpent, saying he made her do it.

FALLOUT FROM THE FALL

All the players in this drama are now present and accounted for. In the next part of this chapter, we see that Satan, having taken the form of a serpent, has shown up for this crucial conversation. We can just imagine Satan's confidence in his victory and his relishing this opportunity to gloat. He would now take over as "the god of this world" (2 Corinthians 4:4) with God's image-bearers under his subjugation. But Satan's seeming victory was not a surprise to God. A sentence of ultimate defeat against Satan reveals God's plan of redemption through the woman. God would have the last word, and Satan would not even be permitted to speak. Instead, God speaks a prophetic judgment on the serpent.

> So the Lord God said to the serpent, "Because you have done this . . . I will put enmity between you and the woman, and between your offspring and hers; he will crush your head, and you will strike his heel." (Genesis 3:14-15)

The seed of the woman would be God's solution to mankind's sin problem and its devastating consequences. Satan's reign of terror, which would subsequently be played out in time and history, would ultimately come to an end. In the meantime, everything in the perfect world God had created would suffer death and decay. And the woman would become a prime target of satanic antagonism. Let's look at the biblical description of this eventuality.

> To the woman he [God] said, "I will make your pains in childbearing very severe; with painful labor you will give birth to children. Your desire will be for your husband, and he will rule over you." To Adam he said, "Because you listened to your wife and ate fruit from the tree about which I commanded you, 'You must not eat from it,' cursed is the ground because of you; through painful toil you will eat food from it all the days of your life". . .
>
> Adam named his wife Eve, because she would become the mother of all the living. The Lord God made garments of skin for Adam and his wife and clothed them. And the Lord God said, "The man has now become like one of us, knowing good and evil. He must not be allowed to reach out his hand and take also from the tree of life and eat and live forever." So, the Lord God banished him from the Garden of Eden to work the ground from which he had been taken. (Genesis 3:16-23)

Note in this passage that the perfect safety and intimacy of the husband-wife relationship has been lost. Adam and Eve are now banished from their garden home where every need had been abundantly provided. Survival would be a struggle in their new hostile environment. How depressing for Adam and Eve to be left alone to face such an unwelcomed future. But take heart that this disturbing scene in human history doesn't end there. Two things happen that lets us know mankind was not left without hope and could take comfort in God's prophetic promise.

Not Without Hope

First, Adam gives his wife the name Eve because she would become "the mother of all living." This affirms that her seed would ultimately give birth to the Savior of the world, the one who would restore the intimate relationships lost to sin. Secondly, God makes garments of skin for Adam and Eve. The phrase "and he clothed them" carries with it a personal, tender expression of God's deep love for them. God knew Adam and Eve would have a difficult time adjusting to the climate and terrain outside the garden. So even after they'd messed up so badly, he makes provision for their comfort.

Let's consider for a moment what sewing clothing of animal skins entails? First, it required the very first animal sacrifice performed by God himself. Being God, he could undoubtedly have skipped all the mess and fuss, not to mention the bloodshed of killing animals for their skins and just spoke their clothing into existence. But the imagery of God making garments of skin to clothe Adam and Eve is a graphic picture of how God would later make provision for all of us. Through the ultimate blood sacrifice of the Lamb of God at Calvary, our nakedness would be clothed with robes of righteousness (Isaiah 61:10). We would be able to make our journey back into the Garden of Eden, representing a full restoration of the broken relationships.

Now let's rewind to Genesis 3:16 to hear God speak a pronouncement over the woman that is pivotal to understanding how the Fall changed everything: "Your desire will be for your husband, and he will rule over you."

It is hard to estimate the magnitude of the cause and effect of this decree. Every man and woman who has ever lived has these words written on the DNA of their hearts. A resounding echo can still be heard today, constantly reminding us of the woman's disobedience. As a woman deeply affected by the results of the Fall, I (Carol) am highly vested in knowing what that pronouncement means.

The standard explanation I've heard over the years is that this verse means women will desire to control men. In fact, the New Living Translation of the verse reads, "And you will desire to control your husband, but he will rule over you."

Based on this interpretation, I've tried to be conscious of ways in which I might be taking control in our marriage. How many of the conflicts Eric and I have had in almost fifty years of marriage had been about my desire to control Eric? What about his desire to control me? Or is there something different about this new arrangement after the Fall we hadn't considered? What is clear is that the perfect relationship between the first man and woman was marred almost beyond recognition.

Chapter Six

Opposing Desires

The account of the Fall in Genesis 3 makes clear that both the man and woman would suffer greatly as two opposing inclinations were introduced into the husband-wife relationship like a life-threatening virus. There are various interpretations of Genesis 3:16 and how those sinful inclinations would show up. While Eric and I (Carol) were conducting a pastor's conference in one Caribbean nation, I asked one leader what Christians in that culture understood Genesis 3:16 (i.e., "the woman will desire her husband") to mean. His response was mystifying. He said it refers to a woman's sexual desire for her husband. He then elaborated that the man in turn was designated by God to "rule over" those desires.

Not surprisingly, Eric seemed to find this interpretation particularly appealing (ha!) as it implied that it was the man's prerogative to regulate the sexual relationship in the marriage, determining when those desires will be fulfilled. In my thinking, this suggested a woman's sexuality was under the man's control and for his satisfaction. While I found this interpretation disturbing, it wasn't something I hadn't encountered before while involved in missions in various developing nations—or for that matter in North American church culture in past generations.

To put it bluntly, sex on demand is expected of the woman. One African Christian publication I read explained why women weren't permitted to wear pants. Not for some notion of modesty or dressing like men, but because a woman must always be easily accessible to her husband whenever he wants sex!

Such blatantly egregious distortions of God's purpose for the marriage relationship captured our (Eric and Carol) interest to uncover what similar distortions have crept into our own local churches. The first such misunderstanding is that "he will rule over her" is an injunction representing God's established order rather than an aberration related to the consequences of sin. Those espousing this also teach that a woman's desire is to control her husband and that sinful disposition must be confronted through the man taking the upper hand in the relationship.

So what exactly is meant in this passage? Only with a proper understanding of both the man's and woman's conflicting desires can we discover what went wrong in their relationship and seek to make it right as it was "from the beginning." After a lifetime of uncertainty on this issue, here is our best understanding as a married couple of what God is saying about the woman and her relationship to the man.

First, the word "desire" does not specifically refer to "control," but is most correctly translated "to turn toward." So if we take this passage at face value, the most straightforward interpretation is that the woman will turn toward her husband in way originally reserved for God. Her prevailing inclination will be to look to her husband for her value and security rather than to God. Keep in mind that throughout virtually the entirety of human history, a woman has literally belonged to her husband as a piece of property, so her only value and security did indeed come from that relationship.

So what is the catch? How is this a judgment and consequence of sin? Simply put, in looking to the man and desiring him as her source of value and security, the woman will turn her focus away from God as her source of life. Doing so leaves her vulnerable to the man's control and abuse. Wendy Alsup, the author of *Practical Theology for Women*, says it very candidly when she writes:

> We are not going to really understand how the gospel equips us to reclaim God's image in us as his daughters until we understand clearly what our problem is. I can't emphasize strongly enough that the problem in women created by the fall is deeper than control and domination . . . Apart from Christ, our tendency after the fall is to set up men as being able to meet needs in us that only God can meet, and there is no limit to how desperate we can become. That is nothing less than idolatry.

THE FINAL DEATH BLOW

After years of misunderstanding this cryptic prophecy from Genesis 3:16, the straightforward interpretation rings true to us. "Your desire will be for your husband" is followed immediately by "and he will rule over you," marking the final death blow to the perfect oneness of their relationship. Both the man and the woman turned their eyes away from God. As a result, they no longer have God as their provider now that "by the sweat of your brow will you have food to eat" (verse 19). The man will look to his wife to serve him and meet his needs from a position of dominance. The woman will look to the man to meet her needs and protect her with his larger, more powerful body against outside dangers and enemies. God's prophetic words "and you shall surely die" finds fulfillment in how fallen men and women would now relate to each other apart from God.

We have only to look at history to see how the relationship between men and women would suffer because of the Fall. Trust would be eroded. Intimacy would be forsaken. Oneness would be unachievable. The demise of marriage and the family as God had envisioned it is documented within the first and second generations of mankind. The sacred union of two becoming one was forsaken as men took multiple wives. Men assumed a position of strength and superiority over women as though some divinely authorized assignment rather than a condition of sin. Women became exploited for sexual gratification and as domestic slaves.

The consequences of these two sinful dispositions within men and women have plagued human history with untold misery. Nor is the horrible fallout from this death blow just a faint memory from past ages since the appalling abuse of women and their depreciation continues even today all over our planet. There are few greater challenges currently beckoning the church's attention than to re-examine our understanding of God's redemptive plan for marriage and its restoration to his original plan.

FALLING OUT OF LOVE

Christian men and women today face the challenge to override their natural inclinations. For men, the temptation is to cling to the sin-won and Satan-celebrated position of dominance over women. For women, the temptation is looking to a man for security and sense of value and attempting to manipulate him to get what she wants. Ladies, we must be aware of wanting to turn toward our husbands in a way that should be reserved for our relationship with God alone. No man was meant to bear the full weight of a woman's needs and expectations. While a woman's dependency on a man may be appealing to him, these misdirected longings are what evoke our tendency to manipulate and control our husband to get our needs met.

This in turn results in perpetuating hurtful relationships that fall short of God's design. So let's look again at just what *is* God's design. To start with, as a relational triune spirit, God does everything motivated by love. In fact, 1 John 4:8 states that "God is love." His most defining essence is love. He desires to showcase this lovingkindness before all creation. As the crown of creation, the man and the woman were God's mirrored image, perfectly reflecting the glory of this divine love.

With this foundational understanding, there are some questions we must ask ourselves. How were God's image-bearers to manifest this love? How was this love meant to define the relationship between the man and the woman? Larry Crabb in his book *Fully Alive: A Biblical Vision of Gender that Frees Men and Women to Live Beyond Stereotypes* responds to this question.

> Each of us as a man or a woman is called by the gospel to find ourselves by losing ourselves in God's love story . . . What we are designed to reveal about God is something that, as gendered image-bearers, we were wired to uniquely enjoy and reveal.

Surely the essence of being female and male must first and foremost be an expression of love and mutuality. Sadly, the teachings of the church have historically emphasized the woman being created for the man to meet his needs and to serve "under" him. Using Scripture to support and mandate the subordination of women to men creates an inaccurate representation of gospel-love in relationships. It hinders intimate relational love from growing and being nurtured. Instead, it can foster self-serving expectations that become demanding and demeaning in the relationship. Love is seeking the best good for another, not looking to benefit ourselves through another person.

FEELING LONELY AND CONFUSED

Eric and I (Carol) would like to share our own experience as a married couple struggling to make sense of the effects of the Fall in our relationship. You could say we experienced what it's like to "fall out of love" in our attempt to conform to the top-down relationship model of Christian patriarchy. This model left us feeling lonely, frustrated, and confused in our marriage.

As a conservative evangelical, I (Eric) had been schooled in the patriarchal tradition that a woman's role was to meet a man's needs as his helper. I found this dogma confusing. But more so, such a belief sacrificed any true loving intimacy and hindered my relationship with Carol from maturing. In social philosophy, "objectification" is a term that describes what happens in a relationship where one person is seen as an object for meeting the needs of the other person. It is part of the process of dehumanization, the act of disavowing the humanity of others.

While this may sound extreme in application to marriage, it is to some extent what happened to us. I looked to Carol to meet my needs, and she looked to me to have her needs met.

Everyone goes into marriage with idealistic hopes and dreams. Disappointment and disillusionment are even more inevitable when extra-biblical roles are imposed on the relationship by the Christian community. Like most men, I came into marriage thinking I was supposed to be the boss, whatever that meant. By temperament I'm not a forceful, demanding person. Growing up, I'd been emotionally wounded by an over-controlling mother, which left me unsure of myself around stronger people, especially women like Carol. So when Carol and I disagreed, I would often react negatively, assuming she was trying to manipulate me into something I felt uncertain about.

As I struggled with an unmet need for unconditional love, I attempted to be more and do more to compensate for my sense of unworthiness. I also felt pressured by Carol's own need for significance. As a woman with the gift of spiritual leadership, she was compelled to look to me to fulfill her calling since in our church culture this could only be achieved vicariously through a man. As a result, I felt immense pressure to become a successful, dynamic spiritual leader at the cost of neglecting my family.

Somewhere along the way, friendship and intimacy in our relationship got lost in a struggle to determine who was supposed to be doing what. To be honest, I didn't really know what was expected of me. What was the "manly" thing to do? How should a man respond when his wife is better at leading in certain areas where you've been taught you're supposed to take the lead? At the time, I believed this to be my assigned role even when I could see that Carol had a clearer perspective in decision-making. This frustration was the direct result of believing that according to the Bible I should always have the last word. You can imagine how depreciating and frustrating it was for Carol!

THE WOMANLY THING TO DO

Conversely, what is the "womanly" thing to do? One mixed message I (Carol now!) heard as a young woman came at a bridal shower from an older woman giving advice to the younger women present. It went something like this: "Don't learn how to do things better than your husband. A man needs to think he knows more than his wife so she will respect him and depend on him. It makes him feel more like a man."

At the time, that all sounded somehow biblical. But it also sounded ridiculous that women were required to act unintelligent and incompetent so men could feel they were in charge. If women already held an inferior position, why are we then required to dumb down even more so men could feel better about themselves? It presented a double bind for me. I could either fully express my

God-given gifts and abilities or depreciate myself so as not to upstage my man or other men for that matter.

I once thought such advice as I received at that bridal shower was well outside the norm even for complementarians. Sadly, I've learned that it is actually widespread. One missionary friend shared how as National Merit Scholarship finalist and top-ranking student in her missionary boarding school graduating class, it was assumed she'd be valedictorian.

Shortly before graduation, she was called to the office, where the male principal explained that as a female it wouldn't be biblical for her to be giving a valedictorian address, especially since the graduation was being held in the school chapel, technically a church where women were to be silent. More significantly, being valedictorian would place her above male classmates, which could negatively impact their "spiritual authority" and self-confidence in their masculinity.

My acquaintance was left wondering why the school permitted high-scoring female students on the honor roll to begin with if it was so unbiblical for male students to know a female had scored higher. Ironically, for that particular class finding a male valedictorian necessitated dropping to the fourth-ranking graduate. Only as an adult in reexamining Scripture for herself did my friend realize how far from God's design this attitude was.

In my own life and marriage, not unlike many young women, I fell prey to the assumption that success meant being what a man wanted or needed me to be. I concluded that if I wanted to secure Eric's love, I would need to learn how to be compliant and conform to his expectations. Unfortunately, what I thought Eric needed me to be was someone very different from whom I was. And though I didn't know it at the time, Eric was just as unsure of what it meant to be a husband as I was to be a wife. We soon learned that fitting into Christian stereotypes would require both of us to be very different people than who we actually were.

It didn't take long in the close confines of marriage for our incompatibilities to show up. My (Carol) assertiveness and intensity didn't fit the "meek and quiet" image often depicted of a godly woman. When I showed up with my drive to be a leader and the inborn competencies accompanying that drive, the sparks would fly. And while Eric had amazing gifts and qualities in his own right, it was easy for him to feel I was challenging his authority. There were times when I failed in my attempts to be compliant and was instead overwhelmed by anger over the inequality of this arrangement.

Our marriage suffered for years due to a lack of understanding God's original design for oneness in marriage. We will share more in later chapters about our struggle to make a marriage work that was based on patriarchy and how we found our way out of that confinement. But we could (and maybe will!) write a book on the issue of marriage alone and how hurtful stereotypical role expectations for men and women can be as they play out in relationships.

Chapter Seven

The Fallen World Social System

Before leaving Scripture's epic accounts of creation and the Fall, let's do a quick overview. We witnessed God's ideal in the first two chapters of Genesis where he creates the man and the women as equals to rule the world with mutuality. After the Fall, we have God's statement to the woman in Genesis 3:16 that "your desire shall be for your husband, and he shall rule over you."

From this point forward, we see historically the man beginning to rule over the woman. We also see women now looking to men for their core identity, value, and security instead of to God. But far from being God's original design in creation, this is a radical departure from God's plan. Behind it all is the satanic inspiration of a new world social system targeting the demise of women and using men's fallen nature to do his bidding. It is within the context of judgment, not creation that the subjugation of women to men begins and the war on women is declared.

The biblical record doesn't conceal or minimize the tragic effects of sin and a world under satanic control. The social and cultural consequences of the Fall didn't take long to have an impact as Scripture gives witness. By Genesis chapter six we see how humanity's condition has deteriorated.

> Now the earth was corrupt in God's sight and was full of violence. God saw how corrupt the earth had become, for all the people on earth had corrupted their ways. (Genesis 6:11-12)

By this point, the dominance of men subjugating women is already ingrained in the very fabric of human society. We see the practice of bigamy (being married to two women at the same time) by the fourth chapter of Genesis. The great patriarch Abraham, father of the nation of Israel, was himself a bigamist. When his wife Sarah failed to conceive, he took his slave Hagar as a concubine to bear him a child (Genesis 16). Abraham's grandson Jacob took bigamy to the next level of polygamy (multiple wives). He had two wives (sisters Leah and Rachel) and two concubines or mistresses (Bilhah and Zilpah), through whom he had twelve sons (Genesis 29-30). As you might imagine, resentment and bitterness between his wives and children were rampant in his household.

Abraham's nephew Lot was visited by two angels sent by God to warn him of the destruction of Sodom and Gomorrah (Genesis 19). When his home was surrounded by a mob of men demanding Lot's visitors be sent out to be raped, Lot refuses and offers the mob his two virgin daughters instead. Judges 19 tells a similar story of a horrific rape and murder of a Levite's concubine, whom the Levite had sent out to be violated by a mob instead of himself. It would seem women, even their own daughters and wives, were expendable to even allegedly devout followers of God!

Bigamy and polygamy continued to be practiced throughout the Old Testament. Women were property of their husbands while daughters could be either sold into slavery to pay off debt or married for a bride price (Genesis 29, Exodus 21:7, Nehemiah 5:5). Marriages were typically arranged by male family members before a girl reached puberty. Women were not allowed to inherit property, only sons. Neither were they taught the Torah. A woman was not allowed to divorce her husband. But a husband could write a certificate of divorce and send his wife from his house if she displeased him (Deuteronomy 24:1).

While the virginity of a young man was considered inconsequential, if a woman failed to bleed on her wedding night, she could be executed on the doorstep of her parents' home (Deuteronomy 22:21). Daughters of priests who engaged in sexual relations outside of marriage were to be burned alive (Leviticus 21:9). Virgins captured in war were considered plunder along with children, livestock, and treasure taken from the besieged city (Numbers 31, Deuteronomy 21). These are just a few snapshots of the consequences of patriarchy recorded in the Bible. The darkness of the portrayal makes it hard to read many parts of the Old Testament that chronicle the spiral downward of humanity's behavior after the Fall.

It is hard to conceive that some Christians believe these Old Testament accounts attest to the supremacy of men and inferior nature of women. Sadly, some of these practices still occur today in certain developing nations. For example, virginity testing of a woman is still being practiced prior to marriage, especially in Muslim nations. In October 2018, the UN Human Rights Council, UN Entity for Gender Equality, and the World Health Organization (WHO) issued a joint statement that virginity testing must end as it is a painful, humiliating, and traumatic practice, constituting violence against women.

Polygamy is also alive and well in our world. A survey of Muslim women reveals how women subjected to polygamy are abusively neglected and left without shelter or financial support. Concubines are also a common practice in many cultures, while even in the so-called "west," married men routinely maintain mistresses, which amounts to the same thing. These are just a few examples, having already cited many other atrocities earlier.

Fallout in the Church

If the witness of Scripture and the global oppression of women still today isn't enough to convince you that patriarchy is a consequence of sin and the Fall, not God's original design for society, we need to look no further than the church. We (Eric and Carol) oppose Christian patriarchy for many reasons as already cited. But not the least is the minimal or no accountability required by hierarchical church structures of male leadership. As only too many recent revelations have made clear, abuse scandals are often swept under the rug because they are adjudicated "in house" by elders or religious leaders who are exclusively male.

When only men have the power to address sinful behavior, objective evaluations of abuse are hard to come by. The result? Male-dominated ministries are often protected from the inside by men who believe defending the ministry is more important than protecting the victims of abuse. While such abuse once thrived in the darkness of secrecy, silencing, and cover-ups, God has shed divine light on the problem of abuse not only in the Catholic church but also among Protestant churches and ministries.

Survivors have spoken out about pervasive abuse or sexual misconduct in ministries such as Sovereign Grace Ministries, Vision Forum, Jesus People USA, the Bill Gothard Ministry, Bob Jones University, Patrick Henry College, Pensacola Christian College, and several missions organizations. Read the reports and weep. Almost all the above-mentioned ministries found guilty of protecting abusers promoted Christian patriarchy. Simultaneously, they ridiculed and demonized egalitarian ideologies while promoting strict gender roles of what biblical manhood and womanhood had to look like.

Carol and I (Eric) were exposed early in our marriage to a teaching that described the family by a series of umbrellas representing biblical authority. First, God holds the largest umbrella. Next was the husband holding an umbrella over his wife and children. Spiritual protection was dependent on staying underneath the authority of the person holding the umbrella over you. We were taught that a woman's spiritual flourishing was determined by her submission to her husband. According to this teaching, the wife needed to make sure she didn't grow or develop beyond what was comfortable for her husband.

Meanwhile, a daughter, regardless of her age, remained under the father's umbrella (authority) until she moved over to the umbrella of her husband at marriage. In addition, verses were used to show how if a woman stepped out from under the umbrella, whatever that exactly looked like, she would be susceptible to satanic attack.

Where does this teaching about umbrellas come from? It's a concept popularized by Bill Gothard, who teaches legalism and promotes authoritarian structures to churches and families through his organization, Institute of Basic Life Principles (see **Understanding "Umbrellas of Protection"** at the IBLP website). Like much problematic teaching, this concept takes biblical principles but then applies them beyond the bounds of Scripture.

The abuse and dysfunction in marriages spawned by this teaching is incalculable. We saw its effects creating confusion in our own marriage relationship as we tried to contort ourselves to fit the model. After all, it was in line with the hierarchal model we'd been taught within the church, so who were we to dare challenge that? While Bill Gothard's teaching has less influence today in the wake of his personal sexual misconduct, we hear the same disturbing tone of legalism and implicit conformity in current complementarian teaching.

The Ultimate Court of Appeal

"Okay, I hear you!" you might be saying about now. "This is all bad news for the church, and it's heartbreaking to hear how women have suffered under the abuse of spiritual authority. But for the Christian community, the ultimate court of appeal must be the Scriptures themselves."

We couldn't agree more! We believe Scripture itself offers a compelling argument that women's subordinate role to men in both the world and the church is not God's idea but fallen man's. Our goal is to present our findings in hopes of bringing about much-needed reform in the Christian community. We may not be able to change overnight this world's satanically inspired social system of patriarchy. But the church has a responsibility to model the radical difference in how Kingdom culture operates.

We want to close this chapter by sharing a famous methodology for theological reflection credited to John Wesley, leader of the Methodist movement in the late eighteenth century. It is called the Wesleyan Quadrilateral. Wesley and other Methodist scholars saw four principle factors that illuminate believers in their quest for truth.

- **Scripture:** The Bible must always be our primary source and standard for Christian doctrine.

- **Tradition:** This consists of the witness of the development and growth of the Christian faith through the past centuries and in many nations and cultures.

- **Reason:** Through reason, the individual Christian applies discernment as well as rational and coherent thought to the Christian faith.

- **Christian Experience:** Experience is the individual believer's understanding and appropriating of the faith in the light of his or her own life and observations.

These four elements taken together bring the believer to a mature and fulfilling understanding of the Christian faith along with the required response of worship and service. In our own quest to understand God's design for womanhood and manhood, we have utilized all four of these elements in evaluating the reliability and truthfulness of biblical egalitarianism versus Christian patriarchy. We invite you to do the same.

PART II:

GOD'S STORY OF WOMANHOOD

"Woman does not possess the image of God in herself . . . but as far as the man is concerned, he is by himself alone the image of God."

—**Saint Augustine**

"Let us make mankind (male and female) in our image, in our likeness, so that they may rule."

—**God**

Chapter Eight

The Weaker Vessel

Depending on where one lives in our global community, there are vastly different perspectives about the value and significance of manhood versus womanhood. In many developing nations across Africa, Asia, and the Middle East where misogynistic patriarchy is unquestionably the dominating culture, women are regarded as significantly inferior to men and treated in like manner. We have given evidence of how patriarchal cultures put women at risk to the abusive domination of men. Most contemporary Christians would believe that women should be regarded with greater respect than we see around the world. At the same time, Christians often ignore the egregious discrimination that has gone unchallenged in the church for centuries.

Blatant Misogyny

In tandem with secular culture, ecclesiastic discrimination against women has been blatantly misogynistic down through the centuries, influencing the church's theology today. John

Chrysostom, Archbishop of Constantinople in the fourth century, believed that God maintained the order of each sex by dividing the business of life into two parts, assigning the more necessary, beneficial aspects to the man and the less important, inferior matters to the woman. Saint Augustine, fourth century church father and to this day arguably one of the most influential theologians in church history, spoke against the clear teaching of Scripture when he wrote:

> Woman was given to man, woman who was of small intelligence and who perhaps still lives more in accordance with the promptings of the inferior flesh than by superior reason. This is why the apostle Paul does not attribute the image of God to her.

Continuing further along the historical path of famous Christian philosophers, we come to Saint Thomas Aquinas, known for his brilliant contributions to theology and doctrine. In the thirteenth century he wrote:

> As regards to the individual nature, woman is defective and misbegotten, for the active force in the male seed tends to the production of a perfect likeness in the masculine sex; which the production of woman comes from a defect.

What about the great sixteenth century church reformer Martin Luther? He said too many derogatory things about women to list. But here are just a few things he believed. He considered women to be less rational than males on a scale in which rational equated with better. Like Eve, women were more easily led astray than men.

Their reasoning faculties were less engaged than men's and less capable of high development. Girls neither required nor could master higher learning so should be limited to schooling that trained them in piety, housekeeping, and upright motherhood. For Luther, a women's anatomy confirmed their created purpose as mothers rather than thinkers, their broad hips designed for giving birth while their narrow shoulders denoted a lack of weight in the upper quarters, i.e., their heads/brains.

In like manner, sixteenth century theologian John Calvin saw women as less than men. In fact, he imputes to women the ruin of the entire human race, going on to state:

> Since the woman seduced the man from God's commandment, it is fitting that she should be deprived of all her freedom and placed under a yoke . . . On this account, all women are born that they may acknowledge themselves as inferior in consequence to the superiority of the male sex. Let the woman be satisfied with her state of subjection, and not take it amiss that she is made inferior to the more distinguished sex.

John Knox, well-known sixteenth century Scottish minister and founder of the Presbyterian Church of Scotland, stated:

> Nature, I say, paints women further to be weak, frail, impatient, feeble and foolish, and experience has declared them to be inconstant, variable, cruel and lacking the spirit of counsel and leadership.

John Wesley eighteenth century founder of the Methodist Church adds to this litany:

> A woman ought not to teach because she is more easily deceived, and more easily deceives.

These convictions held by men looked up to as giants in the Christian faith reflect the patriarchal culture of their day and their own theological ignorance and gender bias. Their perspectives have profoundly affected the lens through which Scripture has been interpreted down through church history. Without depreciating the immense doctrinal contributions of these men, we must not ignore how their distorted view of women is with us today within the conservative evangelical church as well as other denominations.

Misguided Biases

What we (Eric and Carol) have discovered in our research and study of Scripture is that the church today is still plagued by misguided biases. For instance, in I Peter 3:7 women are described as being "weaker" than men.

> Husbands, in the same way be considerate as you live with your wives, and treat them with respect as the weaker partner and as heirs with you of the gracious gift of life, so that nothing will hinder your prayers.

In the King James Version, "weaker partner" is translated as "weaker vessel." In light of the above historical quotes, it is not surprising to see how this verse has routinely been taken out of context and used to profile women as morally and spiritually weaker than men. Which is ironic since an unbiased survey would indicate that men have historically had a greater problem with infidelity and integrity.

The term "weaker vessel" has also been used to suggest women are emotionally and mentally fragile, making them unqualified to hold positions of leadership. That has never made sense to me (Carol) either. In our marriage, Eric is more sensitive and emotional than I am. So does that make him weaker than me or unqualified to be a leader?

Obviously, there are physical differences between men and women. Men are on average one-third to one-half larger, taller, and stronger than women with greater muscle mass than women. That doesn't mean there aren't certain women who are taller and bigger than certain men. But scientifically speaking, women are in fact physically the weaker gender.

Which puts the apostle Peter's teaching here in perspective. He was writing in a culture and historical period when men literally owned their wives, had every legal right to beat them at will, and by their larger mass could inflict major pain and injury on them. So it makes total sense that a first century apostle instructing Christian men on how to treat their wives would include the command to treat them with consideration and respect. This was in contrast to the domestic violence so prevalent and permitted in their society— as it remains in patriarchal societies today.

If we are going to look at definitions of "weaker," we should also include studies that show women have a greater tolerance to pain and physical discomfort (imagine men going through multiple childbirths!). In industrialized nations where other factors are equal, women also tend to outlive men by six to eight years.

But a closer look at 1 Peter 3:7 can give us valuable insights about the husband-wife relationship and what more importantly is meant by "the weaker partner" or "weaker vessel." For starters, it must be put in context with the entire passage, which begins with a similar injunction to the wife on how she should treat her husband.

> Wives, in the same way submit yourselves to your own husbands so that, if any of them do not believe the word, they may be won over without words by the behavior of their wives, when they see the purity and reverence of your lives. (1 Peter 3:1-2)

The instruction here to the wife is that she is to be submissive and respectful to her husband, showing him honor. By law women were already required to submit to husbands as their property and could be punished harshly for doing anything else. The point here is that as Christian women, they weren't to submit simply because they had no alternative, but in such a respectful, loving, honoring way that even if their husbands weren't Christians, they would be drawn to faith by their wife's godly testimony.

Similarly, Christian slaves were admonished to serve their masters sincerely as to Christ, even unjust masters, so not to dishonor God's name (1 Timothy 6:1-2, Ephesians 6:5-8, 1 Peter

2:18). Once again, it isn't as though slaves had any other choice than to serve their masters, nor would any theologian suggest these parallel passages offer approval of slavery (see 1 Corinthians 7:21). But as Christians, the attitude in which they served gave testimony to the life-changing impact of their Christian faith.

THREE GOOD REASONS

Bearing in mind that just as the Christian wife is admonished to honor and respect her husband, so the Christian husband is admonished to respond in like manner to his wife, notice that three reasons are given for why a husband should treat his wife with special consideration and respect. We've already discussed the first, which is because she is "the weaker partner." Secondly, notice that the verse goes on to add that it is because the wife is "heir" with the husband (NIV) or "your equal partner" in the New Living Translation. Here we come back to God's original design for the man and woman in creation, which was to be joint partners with an equal inheritance in God's Kingdom.

The third reason given to the husband for respecting his wife is "so that nothing will hinder your prayers." This is even more significant in the context of when Peter wrote this epistle, since as we've already discussed, women had no choice but to submit to their husbands, on pain of serious punishment. Their only choice was the attitude with which they submitted.

In contrast, the husband had to choose to treat his wife lovingly, and the only person who could hold him accountable for how he treated his wife was God himself. Plainly put, the apostle Peter is telling husbands here (and unlike the apostle Paul, Peter was a married man who traveled in the gospel with his wife; see 1 Corinthians 9:5) that if they don't treat their wives as equals, their relationship with God will be affected negatively, including answer to their prayers. *The Message* paraphrase of this verse supports this perspective.

> As women, they lack some of your advantages. But in the new life of God's grace you're equals. Treat your wives as equals so your prayers don't run aground. (1 Peter 3:7)

In the secular culture at the time the apostle Peter was writing, the Christian husband's responsibility to show his wife honor and respect represented a radical counter-cultural response to how women were typically treated. Women certainly had a "weaker" position than men within the Greco-Roman and Jewish cultures of their day. Because of the disregard and disrespect women faced in the oppressive secular cultures, Christian husbands were being challenged to demonstrate a completely different value system, one reflecting the very honor and respect God himself bestows on women. And it appears that God isn't interested in listening to a man who doesn't treat one of HIS daughters with honor and respect!

The apostle Peter also wants to ensure that Christian men understand the equality of women as "co-heirs of the grace of life," regardless of their actual social status in the patriarchal culture of their day. Husbands were being challenged to model this revolutionary concept in their relationship to their wives.

This gives us a much different takeaway on this passage than what has been traditionally offered that perpetuates a depreciation of women. Sadly, women have been devalued by men and even by themselves because of a superficial understanding of this passage. In fact, the challenge Peter is giving here is for a Christian husband to be careful not to allow the oppressive patriarchal culture all around to affect his relationship to his wife because that in turn will be detrimental to his relationship to God.

THE EQUAL VESSEL

It is possible that I (Carol) have always been an egalitarian at heart even when I wasn't aware of what that meant. I still remember vividly the first time someone said to me, "You're an egalitarian, aren't you?" My answer at the time was an adamant denial. As the pastor's wife, I was expected to support the established tradition that gave men the prominent place of leadership in the home and in the church—and in fact I did.

I don't recall what I'd done or said that prompted a question which to me felt like an indictment. But I do remember rehearsing those words over and over in my mind. An inner agitation had been ignited that I couldn't quite resolve. Was God trying to get my attention? Had I done something wrong? Was who I had become dishonoring to God?

As I mentioned, at the time I wasn't sure what being an egalitarian even meant. I just knew it was related to a view of a woman's role and identity considered contrary to the church's more traditional beliefs. And if I was to be honest with myself, I had to confront questions that had gone unanswered for years. Why are men given preferential status? How is it that women must be granted permission by men to be used by God? Why do men determine what women can and cannot do or be?

I felt incriminated to even entertain these questions. Should I be worried about what this revealed in me? Was this the spirit of rebellion I'd been warned about? The truth was that I never felt I fit into the mold presented by the conservative Christian community in which I'd grown up. I felt a deep call to be a leader, and yet that position appeared to be reserved for men.

As I've previously mentioned, the Bible stories I learned as a child and the sermons I heard on Sunday mornings indicated that God gave men all the important assignments. They were the heroes. Noah obediently built the ark. David undauntedly faced Goliath. Abraham faithfully believed God. Joseph skillfully interpreted the dreams for Pharaoh. Daniel courageously faced the lions when thrown into their den.

Any role a woman played in these stories seemed insignificant if not detrimental to the noble cause of the hero. The very first woman created was deceived by Satan and allegedly caused the man to sin. Sarah was the one who laughed in unbelief at God's promise and offered her slave Hagar to bear Abraham's son. Potiphar's wife tried to seduce Joseph, then lied to her husband, accusing Joseph of rape. Lot's wife looked back at the destruction of Sodom and Gomorrah in violation of the angel's instructions and turned into a pillar of salt. Miriam spoke against Moses and was inflicted with leprosy. Delilah brought Samson to his knees through her deceit. Bathsheba was the seductress causing David to sin. And so on.

There seemed to be an endless list of infamous caricatures of women in the Bible posing as men's biggest problem. Had I missed something in how women are featured in God's story? Were there examples in Scripture of the noble character of women that had been overlooked?

As Eric and I (Carol) dug into Scripture to seek out answers to these questions, we found that the Bible did indeed contain many appearances of women that caused us to think differently of a woman's place in God's story. These were women of remarkable strength to have risen above their disadvantaged position with history-making impact. Fully appreciating their role in God's redemptive plan requires looking at their stories through a different lens than has traditionally been viewed.

These stories also bring into question the limitations imposed on women within the church supposedly based on biblical grounds. Over the next few chapters, we'll take a closer look at a number of these women.

Chapter Nine

Taken by Surprise

Before we dig into the biographies of several remarkable biblical women, here are a few more character assassinations written by historic Christian leaders that will help us to understand the prejudice women have been up against for centuries.

Saint Augustine
Fourth Century Bishop of Hippo

It is the natural order among people that women serve their husbands and children their parents, because the justice of this lies in [the principle that] the lesser serves the greater . . . This is the natural justice that the weaker brain serves the stronger. This therefore is the evident justice in the relationships between slaves and their masters that they who excel in reason, excel in power.

Saint Albertus Magnus
Thirteenth Century Dominican Theologian

> To put it briefly, one must be on one's guard with every woman, as if she was a poisonous snake and the horned devil . . . Thus, in evil and perverse doings woman is cleverer, that is, slyer, than man. Her feelings drive woman toward every evil, just as reason impels man toward all good.

In contrast to these cruel misrepresentations so readily asserted about women, what I (Eric) discovered in my personal study of Scripture took me by surprise. Beginning from Genesis and throughout the Old and New Testament, we find glimpses of God's highly favorable opinion of women and even glorious tributes to their noble character. And though the biblical accounts we have are strongly steeped in a patriarchal culture defined by the Fall, God's redemptive story still reveals God's ultimate vision for his daughters. The door of patriarchy that closed women off from equal partnership with men was never permanently locked.

In fact, it is God himself who opens the door to give women hope for their future redemption and full reinstatement alongside men. Let's begin then in the Old Testament where we can gain greater appreciation for some truly remarkable women who can only be described as unsung heroes of our faith.

Sarah, Mother of Our Faith

The patriarch Abraham, father of the nation of Israel, typically gets the glory for being a man of faith. It's easy to forget that both Abraham and his wife Sarah trusted God together. Abraham and Sarah represent a wonderful picture of biblical partnership. In fact, Sarah is mentioned by name with Abraham in the well-known "roll-call of faith" found in chapter eleven of the New Testament book of Hebrews.

> By faith Sarah herself received power to conceive, even when she was past the age, since she considered him faithful who had promised. (Hebrews 11:11)

This passage makes it clear that Sarah wasn't simply carried along by her husband's faith but had her own. The prophet Isaiah also encourages us to look to Abraham and Sarah as examples of faith.

> Listen to me, you who pursue righteousness, you who seek the Lord: look to the rock from which you were hewn, and to the quarry from which you were dug. Look to Abraham your father *and to Sarah* who bore you. (Isaiah 51:1-2)

When we need hope, we are told here to think about the remarkable legacy of Sarah's faith and perseverance. She was a woman who continued to trust God and ultimately saw the impossible become possible, i.e., the birth of an heir to Abraham when she was ninety years old (Genesis 21). This son of Sarah and

Abraham, Isaac, would not only be the forefather of the nation of Israel but of the promised Messiah, Jesus Christ.

There is another mention of Sarah in the New Testament where she is used as an example for all women to follow. We've already discussed this passage in the apostle Peter's first epistle in context of the first two verses that admonish Christian women on how to honor and respect their husbands and verse seven, which likewise admonishes Christian men on being considerate and respectful to their wives. Sandwiched in between is an interesting description of true feminine beauty, for which Sarah is cited as a prime example.

> Your beauty should not come from outward adornment, such as elaborate hairstyles and the wearing of gold jewelry or fine clothes. Rather, it should be that of your inner self, the unfading beauty of a gentle and quiet spirit, which is of great worth in God's sight. For this is the way the holy women of the past who put their hope in God used to adorn themselves. They submitted themselves to their own husbands, like Sarah, who obeyed Abraham and called him her lord. You are her daughters if you do what is right and do not give way to fear. (1 Peter 3:3-6)

There are two things of note here we would like to address. First, Sarah was a woman of such notable outward beauty that twice she was taken by kings to add to their harem collection (Genesis 12, 20). As wife of a very wealthy man, she certainly had access to fine clothing and jewelry, as we see when Abraham sends off such gifts as a dowry for his son Isaac's bride Rebekah (Genesis 24). So this passage isn't teaching, as has so often been taken out of context, that women shouldn't display any outward beauty by wearing jewelry or fashionable dress.

What these verses do give us is a description of feminine beauty from the inside out that will outlast youthful beauty, that of a meek and quiet spirit, characteristics used to describe Jesus as well. These characteristics are seen in women who have put their hope in God, while showing respect and deference (submission) to their husbands. We know that these same qualities are to be displayed by husbands to their wives as well (v. 7) as previously discussed. Later in the book, we will elaborate in greater depth on the husband/wife relationship where mutual submission is clearly taught as an earmark of the Christian marriage.

And finally, women are told that they are Sarah's daughters, her spiritual heirs, if they follow her example in two areas: 1) doing what is right, and 2) not giving way to fear. We can imagine what kind of fear Sarah must have felt being carried off by strange military forces, thrown into a foreign king's harem, and facing the threat of rape. All while her husband is collecting livestock and servants as gifts from said kings and doing nothing to get her back (unlike a few chapters later when he takes all his men to fight—and win—a war to rescue his nephew Lot).

Instead of giving way to fear, Sarah according to this divinely inspired biography quietly, calmly did what was right and put her hope in God, not her husband (which was just as well since *twice* her husband had failed to rescue her from the harem of the pagan kings; only God's supernatural intervention saved her). God came through for her, not only rescuing Sarah but in the process greatly increasing Abraham's own wealth and prestige. Despite Abraham's admitted failure here as a husband, both Abraham and Sarah are commended for their great faith (Hebrews 11:8-12) and are used by God in his redemptive plan to bring about the nation of Israel and their eventual descendant, Jesus.

RUTH, UNWAVERING COMMITMENT

The story of Ruth is another remarkable character witness to the value and virtue of womanhood. Ruth is a Moabite, who were despised enemies of the Jews. She marries a Jewish man whose family has taken refuge in Moab due to a famine in their own country. When he dies, she finds herself a widow and childless. Without a husband, she is now both destitute and socially disenfranchised. Yet she makes an unprecedented and courageous decision that results in her inclusion into the core biblical cast of redemptive history.

Refusing to abandon her mother-in-law Naomi, Ruth says goodbye to her native land of Moab to accompany Naomi back to Naomi's own homeland of Israel. She leaves her own people and culture to start a new life filled with the certainty of rejection and discrimination. She leaves her own family and religion, rejecting the idols of Moab for the worship of the true God. In her commitment to Naomi, Ruth makes one of the most amazing and courageous statements of faith recorded in Scripture.

> Do not urge me to leave you or to return from following you.
> For where you go, I will go, and where you lodge, I will lodge.

Your people shall be my people, and your God my God. Where you die, I will die, and there will I be buried. May the Lord do so to me and more also if anything but death parts me from you. (Ruth 1:16, 17)

Wow! That commitment was so powerful and irreversible it has rightfully found its way into numerous wedding vows, including the ones Carol and I (Eric) made to each other many years ago.

In the providence of God, Ruth finds favor in the eyes of Boaz, a Jewish landowner who is a close relative of Naomi. Through her marriage to Boaz, Ruth fulfills her commitment to Naomi and establishes her place in the royal lineage of the Messiah. A son born to this divinely selected couple becomes the grandfather of King David and ancestor of Jesus (Matthew 1:3-6). Once a foreigner from an idol-worshipping nation, Ruth is now grafted into the family of God and a mother in Israel. In the end, Ruth becomes one of just two books of the Bible named after a woman.

ABIGAIL, NOBLER THAN NABAL

The story of Abigail and her husband Nabal is certainly one of the more uncommon stories found in Scripture. You could even call it an ancient rendition of "Beauty and the Beast." In 1 Samuel 25:3, Abigail is described as an "intelligent and beautiful woman." The Hebrew word here for intelligent literally means "good in understanding." In other words, she was wise and insightful. The name Abigail literally means "she whose father is (filled with) joy." So she would appear to have been a delight to everyone in her life except for her own husband, Nabal.

In contrast to Abigail, he was a stubborn, selfish, harsh man, ungrateful and unreasonable in his dealings with others. The account in 1 Samuel 25 centers around the time period when David, soon to be crowned king of Israel, was a fugitive from his predecessor King Saul. David and his men had provided protection for the flocks of Nabal and other wealthy landowners from raiders and bandits. Now they needed food, so David requested that Nabal give them some provisions as compensation. When Nabal rudely refuses, David is so insulted that he imprudently gathers his four hundred armed warriors with the intent to destroy Nabal and his entire household.

Abigail comes to the rescue of both men, saving her entire household from disaster while also saving David from a thoughtless act of violence. First, without telling Nabal she immediately puts together a caravan of supplies for David and his men. Then she approaches David and with great diplomacy apologizes for her husband's behavior.

> Please pay no attention, my lord, to that wicked man Nabal. He is just like his name—his name means Fool, and folly goes with him . . . And let this gift, which your servant has brought to my lord, be given to the men who follow you. (1 Samuel 25:25-27).

Abigail certainly contradicts what the patriarchal culture of her time would have expected of her. Instead of submitting to her husband and supporting his destructive stupidity, she takes immediate action. It couldn't have been without risk for her to confront a very angry David and four hundred of his warriors. Far from any indication that Abigail was doing wrong in defying her husband, the biblical account shows David recognizing that Abigail was a divine messenger sent by God to save him from a most regrettable action.

> David said to Abigail, "Praise be to the Lord, the God of Israel, who has sent you today to meet me. May you be blessed for your good judgment and for keeping me from bloodshed this day and from avenging myself with my own hands. Otherwise, as surely as the Lord, the God of Israel, lives, who has kept me from harming you, if you had not come quickly to meet me, not one male belonging to Nabal would have been left alive by daybreak." (1 Samuel 25:32-34)

Abigail eventually becomes David's wife after her husband Nabal was struck down by God for his wicked behavior (1 Samuel 25:38). Abigail demonstrates the rewards that can come to a woman who in the words of the apostle Peter chose to "obey God rather than men" (Acts 5:29). She was ultimately recognized as wise for her unwillingness to submit to an ungodly man's sinful and destructive demands. She provides an example of true godliness and submission to women who have been unfairly intimidated by the misguided teaching of masculine superiority of men over women and husbands over wives.

Esther, Courage Personified

The Old Testament book of Esther, the second of two books of the Bible named after women, is not about a fairytale romance between a king and the winner of a beauty contest. Rather, it describes a horrific and intolerable abuse of women and how one young Jewish girl risked her life to save her people, eventually rising to a position of power and leadership over an entire kingdom.

The time period in question was the Jewish exile and captivity after the fall of Jerusalem. Esther as well as Mordecai, her guardian and uncle, were members of the Jewish community in exile in the city of Susa, capital of the Persian empire. Esther is initially taken to the palace of King Xerxes along with many other virgin young women as part of a nationwide "contest" for the king to choose a new queen (Esther 2). Unlike various movies and fictional depictions of the story, King Xerxes was not a dashing young prince but a wicked and depraved pagan king. And Esther's experience was certainly not one of romantic love but of sexual indulgence and exploitation.

Each of the young women chosen spent a year preparing to spend a single night with the king. Here is how the biblical account describes these encounters.

> In the evening she would go there and in the morning return to another part of the harem to the care of Shaashgaz, the king's eunuch who was in charge of the concubines. She would not return to the king unless he was pleased with her and summoned her by name.

Notice that if Xerxes didn't choose the girl as queen, her fate was to become a permanent sexual slave (concubine) in the king's harem, not even seeing the king again unless she was memorable enough for the king to summon her for a night's pleasure. And it should also be noted that this group of girls weren't the only ones rounded up for the king's pleasure. We read in Esther 2:19 after Esther had already been crowned queen that "when the virgins were assembled a second time, Mordecai was sitting at the king's gate." Even though King Xerxes now had Esther as queen, it didn't abate his lustfulness and a second collection of virgins were assembled for his ongoing sexual gratification.

As the story continues, we meet one of the Jewish people's greatest enemies, a man named Haman. Inspired by Satan, Haman hatches a plan to destroy the entire Jewish race. Once Esther becomes aware of Haman's evil plan, she might have simply ignored the impending genocide. After all, she was safe, secure, and living a life of luxury. But she courageously chose to ignore the danger, risking her comfort, luxury, and even her life to bring deliverance to her people.

Esther was a woman who did have authority over men and could issue commands that were carried out.

> So Queen Esther, daughter of Abihail, along with Mordecai the Jew, wrote with full authority to . . . establish these days of Purim at their designated times, as Mordecai the Jew and Queen Esther had decreed for them . . . Esther's decree confirmed these regulations about Purim, and it was written down in the records. (Esther 9:29-32)

The impact of Esther's courageous heroism is seen to this day through the celebration of Purim, observed annually by the Jewish people. It commemorates the great deliverance God granted the Jews at the hands of Esther and her uncle Mordecai. The message of Esther's life is clear. God uses both men and women in position of authority throughout redemptive history to bring his purposes to pass.

Chapter Ten

God-Sanctioned Authority Over Man?

The biblical women we've looked at thus far have clearly demonstrated tremendous character and courage. As we continue our study of women in the Old Testament, we turn our focus to some women who break even further from the stereotypical complementarian mold. Beginning with one of the most specific biblical examples of a woman being given authority and leadership over men. It is impossible to overemphasize the implications of her life and its relevance to the discussion of women in Christian leadership today.

Deborah, Noble Warrior Hero

The story of Deborah brings to mind the heroine from the recent blockbuster film, Captain Marvel, where she describes herself as a "noble warrior hero." In Deborah's case, we aren't talking about a fictional super-hero but a real-life historical person.

> Now Deborah, a prophet, the wife of Lappidoth, was leading Israel at that time. She held court under the Palm of Deborah between Ramah and Bethel in the hill country of Ephraim, and the Israelites went up to her to have their disputes decided. (Judges 4:4-5)

In just two short verses, we learn that Deborah was a leader of Israel and a prophet who spoke on behalf of God. Though she was married, her husband Lappidoth was clearly not the man in charge. She was a judge, the only leaders Israel had at that time in the nation's history (Gideon, Samson, and Samuel are some other examples). She held court at a specific location, the Palm of Deborah, and people from all over Israel traveled there to have her judge their disputes or problems.

The passage above makes it clear that Deborah is exercising both *spiritual* and *judicial* authority in Israel. We know this because she is declared to be both a prophet and a judge. This is a critical point of clarity because some have suggested that Deborah was only a "civil" leader and not someone who exercised spiritual authority over men. This interpretation is an attempt to reconcile the story of Deborah with the apostle Paul's alleged prohibition against a woman exercising authority over a man.

> I do not permit a woman to teach or to exercise authority over a man; rather, she is to remain quiet. (1 Timothy 2:12)

But as one can readily see in the Judges 4 account, the attempt to bifurcate these two roles, "civil" versus "spiritual," makes absolutely no sense. The amazing example of Deborah as both a spiritual and civil leader is clearly on display here. This creates a problem for the traditional interpretation of 1 Timothy 2:12, since God had already permitted such an exercise of authority here in Judges 4.

We are further told that God in his mercy "raised up judges who saved them [Israel]" (Judges 2:16). And again in 2 Samuel 7:7, we are told that it was God himself who commanded the judges of Israel to "shepherd his people." This means that Deborah was appointed by God to do the things she did. Obviously, Paul is not prohibiting all women in all circumstances from exercising authority over men since God himself gives us a dramatic example of that very thing happening.

Nor does Deborah stop at being a prophet and judge. As the story continues, she calls for Barak, a commander of Israel's armed forces, and gives him God's instructions to go to war against an enemy army (Judges 4:6-8). It doesn't even occur to Barak to question Deborah's authority to speak on behalf of God. But he does insist that she go with his army, refusing to go without her, so that they are assured of having God's presence and authority on the battlefield. Which subsequently makes Deborah the commander-in-chief of Israel's army.

It is worth noting here as well the extensive parallels in leadership between Deborah and Moses. In comparing Exodus 14-18 with Judges 4-5, we see that Moses and Deborah both functioned as judges, were both prophets who proclaimed the word of the Lord, both pronounced blessings and curses, both led military generals (Joshua/Barak), and both led the people in worshipping

God after God gave them a great deliverance. And like Moses, it is clear that Deborah's authority came directly from God himself.

Because of the indisputable and overwhelming evidence supporting Deborah's leadership, some have claimed that she only represents an anomaly. An exception to God's rule that only men should be leaders over other men. They suggest that Deborah must have represented God's "second best" because none of the men of Israel, including Deborah's husband, would step up to lead. This is sometimes referred to as the "Deborah Principle."

The problem with this interpretation is that the story of Deborah gives no indication that God's first choice was a man who declined the position, thus making it necessary for God to move on to a woman. Not to mention this would imply that *all* the men of Israel had declined the position for God to settle on a woman. Including their acclaimed war hero Barak, who in the biblical account is clearly a devoted follower of the LORD.

Deborah's position of authority as a woman may be unusual and somewhat exceptional in biblical history. At the same time, she is a positive example of God's intention to use godly and qualified women to exercise authority over men and nations. Deborah stands in absolute contrast to the claim that women are prohibited by God from exercising authority over men in the church.

Miriam, Moses's Deliverer

It's easy to think of the second book in the Bible, Exodus, as the story of one man. And certainly as Israel's celebrated deliverer, Moses is the central character and one of the greatest leaders in the

Old Testament as well as in human history. But his success was not due to his own calling and leadership alone. He was protected and assisted by several courageous women whose role in his life story is frequently overlooked.

First, we encounter two Hebrew midwives, Shiphrah and Puah, who because they "feared God" (Exodus 1:17, 21) were willing to risk their lives by defying the Pharaoh's command to kill all Hebrew male children. Next, we see Moses's mother Jochebed (Numbers 26:59), whom God used providentially to protect her son. She too disobeyed the Pharaoh's edict by hiding her son for three months before placing him in a basket among the reeds along the bank of the Nile River. In both examples, we see God using courageous women to protect Moses and bring his sovereign will to pass.

Ultimately, the most influential woman in Moses's life proved to be his older sister Miriam. We first meet her as a young girl watching over her baby brother as he floats among the reeds. Even as a young girl, Miriam was tasked with protecting her brother. It was here along the banks of the Nile that Pharaoh's daughter found Moses and had pity on him. At the moment he was lifted from the Nile, Miriam boldly approached Pharaoh's daughter to suggest her own mother as the baby's wet-nurse (Exodus 2:7-9). Miriam not only saved Moses's life that day but also paved the way for the deliverance of Israel.

We don't encounter Miriam again for eighty years. In fact, not until after Israel successfully passes through the Red Sea, when Miriam leads the Israelites in celebration for God's great deliverance. By this time Miriam appears to have become a significant partner in providing leadership for Israel with both her brother Moses and Aaron.

> Then Miriam the prophet, Aaron's sister, took a timbrel in her hand, and all the women followed her, with timbrels and dancing. Miriam sang to them: "Sing to the Lord, for he is highly exalted. Both horse and driver he has hurled into the sea." (Exodus 15:20-21)

Miriam's designation here as a prophet is a significant endorsement. We don't know precisely how or when she became such an important spiritual force in Israel, but it's clear she was one. She has heard God's voice, carried his message to the people, and spoken on his behalf. A later prophet, Micah, confirms this.

> For I brought you up from the land of Egypt and redeemed you from the house of slavery, and I sent before you Moses, Aaron, and Miriam. (Micah 6:4)

How about that? Miriam was clearly not an afterthought in God's plan of redemption. Rather, she was given authority by God to participate in leadership at the highest level possible.

Huldah, The Disenfranchised Prophet

How many sermons have you ever heard about Huldah? Probably not many. In fact, you might not even recognize the name. Her story isn't one commonly taught in Sunday school.

Even so, Huldah is one of the prophets mentioned in the Old Testament as a contemporary of Jeremiah, Zephaniah, Nahum, and Habakkuk. We find her story in two separate books of the Old Testament (2 Kings 22:14-20, 2 Chronicles 34:22-28). The context of the story is the reforms of godly king Josiah, who finds a copy of God's law that the people of Israel have stopped following.

> Hilkiah the priest, Ahikam, Akbor, Shaphan and Asaiah went to speak to the prophet Huldah . . . She said to them, "This is what the Lord, the God of Israel, says: Tell the man who sent you to me, 'This is what the Lord says: I am going to bring disaster on this place and its people, according to everything written in the book the king of Judah has read." . . . So they took her answer back to the king. (2 Kings 22:14-20)

The rest of Huldah's prophecy assures King Josiah that because of his repentance and reform, God's judgement will not come on Israel during his lifetime. Notice that like Deborah, Huldah prophesies with authority and preaches the word of God to a group of men who were seeking her counsel. In this group were men holding the highest civic and religious positions in the country, including the high priest.

Not surprisingly, there are those who as with Deborah try to minimize Huldah's position as prophet by claiming that their ministry was private, not public. But the biblical account doesn't bear that out. Huldah was certainly one of the most influential prophets of her time. Her ministry during the reign of King Josiah influenced one of the greatest renewal movements in Israel's history. Under the leadership of King Josiah and in response to Huldah's prophecy, we are told:

> Josiah removed all the detestable idols from all the territory belong to the Israelites and had all who were present in Israel served the Lord their God. As long as he lived, they did not fail to follow the Lord, the God of their ancestors. (2 Chronicles 34:33)

While Huldah's story is brief, one important detail should be noted. She preaches a sermon. She declares the word of the Lord. This was not just sharing the word at a women's retreat. Her audience was exclusively men. Men who had come to her to find direction from God. Huldah held a respected position of spiritual leadership in Israel and taught the word of God to high-ranking, powerful men. She was clearly a spiritual leader of spiritual leaders.

WOMEN ARE WARRIORS TOO

As a young teen, I (Carol) remember my fascination with the story of Joan of Arc. I was disenchanted by portrayals of girls as superficial and insecure, craving the attention of boys for validation and a sense of importance. Girls were the ones standing on the sidelines at sporting events, scantily dressed and chanting silly rhymes, while boys were out in the arena doing the main thing. Joan of Arc's courage and devotion to God gave me a very different perspective of what it meant to be a woman.

As a peasant girl living in medieval France, Joan of Arc believed that God had chosen her to lead France to victory in its long-running war with England. With no military training, she convinced the embattled crown prince Charles of Valois to allow her to lead a French army to the besieged city of Orleans. A momentous victory over the English was achieved. Several additional swift victories led to Charles VII's coronation at Reims. This long-awaited event boosted French morale and paved the way for the final French victory.

But as history documents, on May 23, 1430, Joan of Arc was captured and handed over to the English, eventually to be burned at the stake at just nineteen years of age. She is quoted to have said, "I am not afraid. I was born to do this." Her demise sounds dreadful and hard to even imagine. Nonetheless, her courage inspired me much as men have been inspired by the story of William Wallace as depicted in the movie *Brave Heart*.

Today Disney, Pixar, Marvel, and other filmmakers are capturing the hearts of young girls with spirited female heroines. Girls can admire the likes of Moana, Belle, Elsa, Ariel, and Merida. They can be inspired by Wonder Woman, Captain Marvel, and Super Girl. All these films are providing young girls with a healthy dose of family-friendly feminist themes. While some Christians express concern about how these young heroines convey an attitude of self-will, defiance, and rebellion, shouldn't we be asking ourselves: what is the church doing to bring to life the amazing stories of women featured in God's epic story of redemption? What feminine heroines are we presenting to compete for the hearts of our girls?

While Hollywood is defining feminine strength with animation and Sci-Fi, we have the opportunity to stagger the imaginations of girls and young women with real-life biblical role models who can encourage them to take a lead role in advancing the Kingdom of God on earth.

While we see God using women significantly throughout Scripture, we often neglect to calculate the implications for how God still wants to use women today. The stories of both male and female heroes of God need to be told in the church today so that the next generation can be inspired and so both young girls and boys can grow up with mutual respect and admiration for God's great servants of both genders.

Chapter Eleven

A Game-Changer for Women

As the apostle Paul wrote to the Galatian church, when Christ stepped out of eternity into time, he turned everything around for women, giving them full status of first-born sons with all the privileges related to this new-found identity.

> But when the set time had fully come, God sent his Son, born of a woman, born under the law, to redeem those under the law, that we might receive adoption to sonship. Because you are his sons, God sent the Spirit of his Son into our hearts, the Spirit who calls out, "*Abba*, Father." So you are no longer a slave, but God's child; and since you are his child, God has made you also an heir. (Galatians 4:4-7)

What a radical concept Jesus modeled in his messianic mission! Furthermore, he commissioned his disciples, both men and women, to follow his example. They were to flesh out this new arrangement of sonship and mutuality in how the church and family would function.

Those of us in twenty-first century westernized cultures can easily miss the significance of how radical the change was for women because Jesus came. In contrast, many women in certain developing world cultures today understand full well the implications of having the status of "sonship." Being a son rather than a daughter can mean the difference between life and death. In God's family, a woman now receives a full portion of the inheritance just like a man. The "adoption to sonship" means that a woman no longer lives with the shame of being worth less than a man. In Christ and through the revelation of the gospel, everything has changed.

To fully understand what a game changer Jesus was for the status of women, let's take a brief look at Judaism during the time of Christ. Based on the command in Deuteronomy 4:9 to "teach them to thy sons," rabbis excluded women from learning the Law of Moses. While the study of Scripture was regarded as extremely important for men, women weren't even allowed to study the sacred texts. Rabbi Eliezer, a first-century teacher of Jewish law, is noted for saying, "Rather should the word of the Torah be burned than entrusted to a woman." Further, the Talmud says, "It is foolishness to teach Torah to your daughter" (Sotah 20a).

Orthodox Jewish men still pray every morning the Talmudic prayer of "gratitude" written by male rabbis nearly two thousand years ago:

> Blessed are you, HaShem, King of the Universe, for not having made me a gentile. Blessed are you, HaShem, King of the

Universe, for not having made me a slave. Blessed are you, HaShem, King of the Universe, for not having made me a woman.

It is of course no surprise that the men who wrote and recited this prayer were grateful not to be women. Men had more personal, social, economic, and spiritual freedom. By Talmudic traditions, respectable women were expected to stay within the confines of their home. The concept of *tzenuah*, or the private role of the woman, was based on Psalm 45:13: "The king's daughter is all glorious within..."

While a man's primary responsibility was public, a woman's life was confined almost entirely *within* the private family sphere. In fact, the terminology for a prostitute was "one who goes abroad." A first century woman of good class didn't even do her own shopping except when accompanied by a slave.

In Judaism, a woman was unapologetically viewed as inferior to a man. She was expected to serve her husband, raise children, and care for her household—period! All the while being aware that at any moment her husband could easily divorce her while she had no right to divorce him in turn. Women rarely owned or inherited property and were not considered reliable witnesses in court. Women weren't even permitted to speak to men in public. Like children, women were to be seen and not heard. And in fact, they were to be seen as little as possible.

Into this patriarchal culture came Jesus Christ, a conspicuous contradiction to the prevailing norms of his day. Jesus spoke to women publicly. He shocked his contemporaries by relating to women with a remarkably high level of respect and value. He shared profound theological truths with them. He granted them accessibility to his inner circle of disciples and invited them to become his disciples as well. Jesus received their support for his ministry.

Ignoring the prejudice, sexism, and misogyny of his day, Jesus chose instead to liberate women and elevate them to an equal standing with men. He allowed women to minister to him and intimately express their affection for him (see the story of the woman who anointed his feet with expensive perfume in Matthew 26:7, Luke 7:37, Mark 14:3). A woman suffering from an issue of blood that made her ceremonially unclean received a healing from Jesus by touching his cloak (Matthew 9:20-22). With utmost compassion, Jesus performed one of his greatest miracles in raising a widow's son from the dead, saving her from almost certain destitution (Luke 7:11-15).

JESUS PARTNERS WITH WOMEN

Jesus gave his very life for women so that they could become "the sons of God" (Galatians 3:26; 4:6) and be fully included in the new covenant community of God's people, the church. He confronted both the Jewish and Gentile world of his day with a new ethic and theology regarding women, proof of which can be seen in the prominent role women played in his earthly ministry. In fact, nothing in the whole of Jesus's public ministry, words, or deeds indicated any effort to restrict the spiritual service of women. The way Jesus treated women revealed God's heart toward his precious daughters, who along with men reflect his divine image to the world.

Since the Gospels focus primarily on the twelve original disciples, who were all men, it is easy to miss just how many women played strategic roles in Jesus's ministry. We must keep in mind that there were many other disciples, including at least seventy Jesus sent out two by two (Luke 10:1) and at least one-hundred-twenty by Pentecost. This is evidenced since there were that many gathered in a single prayer meeting after Jesus's ascension, "including the women and Mary the mother of Jesus" (Acts 1:14).

Female disciples mentioned by name in the Gospels include Mary Magdalene, Joanna the wife of Chuza, manager of Herod's household, Susanna, along with "many" other unnamed women (Luke 8:2-3), Mary the wife of Clopas (John 19:25), Mary and Martha, two sisters from Bethany (Luke 10:38-42). And of course, Mary mother of Jesus and Mary's sister, who was with her at the cross (John 19:25). In fact, the Gospels are replete with instances of "many women" accompanying Jesus throughout his travels. Even after the crucifixion, we see their integral role.

> The *women* who had come with Jesus from Galilee followed Joseph and saw the tomb and how his body was laid in it. Then they went home and prepared spices and perfumes. But they rested on the Sabbath in obedience to the commandment. (Luke 23:55-56)

Women were indispensable to Jesus's ministry, mission, and life. Let's take a close look at just five of these remarkable female disciples.

Mary Magdalene

Mary Magdalene is mentioned more than a dozen times in the New Testament as a prominent disciple of Jesus, and yet historically she has been one of the Bible's most misunderstood characters. She has often been portrayed as a sinful woman and was ultimately described as a prostitute by Pope Gregory I in 591 AD, though scriptural mentions of her give no such indication. It wasn't until 1969 that this error was corrected by the Catholic Church. In 1988, Pope John Paul II in an apostolic letter refers to Mary Magdalene as "the apostle to the apostles" because she was the first messenger (*apostolos*) sent to the apostles to tell them of Jesus's resurrection (John 20:17).

Unfortunately, by the time these corrections were made, false characterizations of Mary Magdalene were widespread both in and out of the church. From medieval art and church writings to novels, modern movies, and even TV programs, she has been misrepresented as seductress and prostitute all the way to being Jesus's wife or mistress.

So who exactly was Mary Magdalene? The one fact we do know from Luke 8:2 is that Jesus had delivered her from seven demons. Beyond that, we find her listed as one of various women who travelled with Jesus and used their own resources to help Jesus and his disciples (Luke 8:1-3). We also see her with other female disciples at the crucifixion.

> Many women were there, watching from a distance. They had followed Jesus from Galilee to care for his needs. Among them were Mary Magdalene, Mary the mother of James and Joseph, and the mother of Zebedee's sons. (Matthew 27:55-56)

> Some women were watching from a distance. Among them were Mary Magdalene, Mary the mother of James the younger and of Joseph, and Salome. In Galilee these women had followed him and cared for his needs. Many other women who had come up with him to Jerusalem were also there. (Mark 15:40-41)

It is also to Mary Magdalene and other women that the first news of Jesus's resurrection is given. Returning to the tomb to anoint Jesus's body, they find it empty. Told by two angels that Jesus has risen from the dead, they report the good news to the disciples.

> They returned from the tomb and reported all these things to the eleven and to all the rest. Now they were Mary Magdalene and Joanna and Mary the mother of James; also, *the other women* with them were telling these things to the apostles. But these words appeared to them as nonsense, and they would not believe them. (Luke 24:9-11)

The apostles' disbelief of the women's report could almost be humorous if it didn't indicate once again the cultural attitude toward the value of a woman's words. Mary Magdalene was also the first eye witness of Jesus's resurrection (John 20:2, 11-18). When she encounters Jesus outside the tomb, he speaks her name, Mary, and she responds with "Rabboni," meaning my master-teacher. In this simple exchange, we see a powerful sense of connection and affection.

Mary Magdalene certainly was one of Jesus's foremost disciples. Her sacrificial and faithful support for his ministry is unquestionable. Her courage in following Jesus right up until his death when many male disciples had run away is a witness to her strength and commitment. That she was the first person to witness the resurrection and be subsequently sent as an "apostle to the apostles" should cause us to pause and reconsider how God might want to use women today to proclaim the gospel.

Mary, the Mother of Jesus

Growing up, I (Carol) understood nothing of Jesus's messianic mission to change the status of women. I remember wondering why Jesus always seemed to select men for all the important assignments. I wanted Jesus to select me to do something brave and noble for him, but I was just a girl. I would imagine myself sitting at his feet and raising my hand to ask, "But what about me?"

To resolve my disappointment, I conjured up a rather ill-conceived idea (keep in mind I was very young or you might think I was suffering from a narcissistic personality disorder!) Rather than imagining myself as a super-hero or Disney princess, I decided I'd volunteer to be the mother of Jesus when he returned. Other than Jesus himself, I couldn't think of anyone more important to be.

I'd learned in Sunday School that Jesus came into the world the first time through a willing young virgin named Mary. I too was willing. I just needed to figure out what it meant to be a virgin and if it was okay that my name was Carol instead of Mary.

My opportunity came one December Sunday morning when my Sunday school teacher was reading us the Christmas story. I felt my heart pounding as she came to the part about Mary being a virgin. This was my chance to have my questions answered. Raising my hand, I blurted before the teacher could acknowledge me, "What is a virgin?"

My teacher's hesitation and the look on her face were clues that my question was stupid and inappropriate. I had visions of spending a lifetime sitting in the corner wearing a dunce cap. Or being banned from Sunday school and forced to sit with my parents in adult church.

But the teacher just told me I needed to ask my parents when I went home. Having just been overwhelmed by shame, I wasn't about to ask them. Besides, the name Carol probably disqualified me anyway. I would have to deal with my dissatisfaction with the limitations of being a girl some other way.

Still, when we read the story of Mary, what girl wouldn't want to be her? The angel Gabriel, when he announces that Mary will be mother of the Messiah, describes her as blessed and favored by God: "Greetings, O favored one, the Lord is with you" (Luke 1:28). And not just because of her special role as mother of Jesus. She is highly honored because of her faith and her willingness to put her faith into action. Though she is "greatly troubled" and "perplexed" at Gabriel's astonishing announcement (Luke 1:29), she responds with courage, and submission to God's will: "Behold, I am the servant of the Lord; let it be to me according to your word" (Luke 1:38).

Mary's initial feelings were well warranted considering the social rejection she and the baby would be up against if she gave birth to what would be considered an illegitimate child. Mary's relative Elizabeth, mother of John the Baptist, later affirms the exceptionality of Mary's faith: "Blessed is she who has believed that the Lord would fulfill his promises to her" (Luke 1:45).

Fast forward more than thirty years to a conversation between Mary and her son Jesus at a wedding in Cana of Galilee (John 2). The host had run out of wine to serve the wedding guests, and Mary appeals to Jesus to solve the problem. Jesus hasn't yet begun his public ministry and doesn't immediately consent. In anticipation of a miracle, Mary simply says to the servants, "Do whatever he tells you" (John 2:5). Jesus instructs the servants to fill six large stone jars with water, resulting in approximately one-hundred-twenty gallons of the best wine ever served at a wedding. In modern terms, this would be the equivalent of about a thousand bottles of wine.

Mary's participation in what John's gospel calls "the first of his [Jesus] signs" (2:11) is enigmatic to say the least. While millions of people worldwide venerate Mary and pray to her for help, protection, and guidance, she points all of us in a very different direction. Mary's final words need to be heeded by all sincere believers. We are to do whatever *he*, Jesus, tells us to do.

Mary not only gave this advice but lived it out herself. The last time she is mentioned in the Bible is at the formation of the early church, where she is listed as one of Jesus's own disciples.

> All these [the apostles] with one accord were devoting themselves to prayer, together with the women and Mary, the mother of Jesus, and his brothers. (Acts 1:14)

There is no doubt that Mary's faith and influence were a powerful force and example in the early church.

MARY AND MARTHA

In Luke 10:38-42, we are given a snapshot of two very close friends of Jesus, sisters Mary and Martha. In a seemingly inconsequential dialogue with Martha, we see Jesus revealing his new priority for women and calling them out of their restrictive and customary roles.

> As Jesus and his disciples were on their way, he came to a village [Bethany] where a woman named Martha opened her home to him. She had a sister called Mary, who sat at the Lord's feet listening to what he said. But Martha was distracted by all the preparations that had to be made. She came to him and asked, "Lord, don't you care that my sister has left me to do the work by myself? Tell her to help me!" "Martha, Martha," the Lord answered, "you are worried and upset about many things, but few things are needed—or indeed only one. Mary has chosen what is better, and it will not be taken away from her."

Perhaps you've heard sermons chiding Martha for being too busy to spend time with Jesus. But there is something far more to be seen in this passage. A generous and godly woman, Martha had welcomed Jesus and his disciples into her home and appears to be working hard to prepare them a meal. Hospitality is a central part of Middle Eastern culture, and Martha was appropriately doing everything in her power to be the consummate host. She was doing a good thing, the anticipated thing, and Jesus's response was not that Martha was doing something wrong.

But Mary had chosen something of even greater importance. She was seated at Jesus's feet listening to him teach. This means she was probably in the part of the house designated for men only (as remains the custom today in parts of North Africa and the Middle East). Sitting at someone's feet was the usual posture of a disciple as the apostle Paul described his own learning experience.

> I am a Jew, born in Tarsus in Cilicia, but brought up in this city, educated at the feet of Gamaliel according to the strict manner of the law of our fathers. (Acts 22:3)

By sitting alongside the men, Mary had assumed the role of a disciple, a role Jesus refused to deny her. Though what she was doing appears culturally inappropriate, Jesus affirmed her, making clear to Martha (and all women) that Mary's choice to be a disciple of Jesus and learn from him would not be taken from her.

To a first-century reader of John's Gospel, the idea of Mary sitting at Jesus's feet among the men rather than being in the kitchen with the other women would have seemed most improper.

I (Carol) have witnessed how this still plays out even today in many cultures. While in Africa for an extended period, I tried several times to persuade my assistant, a well-educated African woman and definitely not someone to be regarded as a servant, to join me at dinner with our male host. I finally came to understand that in her particular culture to eat with us would have been considered disrespectful. Men (and honored foreign female guests like me!) were always served first in the main dining room while women ate afterwards in the kitchen. If I wanted my assistant's company for a meal, I would need to join her in the kitchen. Which indeed I often did.

This may have been what really bothered Martha. While we can't know exactly what is going on in this exchange, it is possible Martha was less upset about the extra work as Mary's immodesty by having intruded into a man's world. It is very likely some of the other male disciples supported Martha's protest. Jesus's response to Martha becomes a monumental teaching moment for the men in the room as well as Mary and Martha. In endorsing Mary's right to be there, Jesus is standing in deliberate opposition to the Jewish culture that permitted only men to receive religious training.

There was only one purpose for a disciple to receive instruction from a rabbi, and that was to follow in his footsteps to become a teacher. At the end of his ministry, Jesus commissions both male and female disciples, instructing them to wait in Jerusalem for the gift of the Holy Spirit (Luke 24:49). The Spirit would empower them to prophesy and proclaim the message of the Kingdom of God. We see this event described in Acts 2 where the Holy Spirit descends upon a room filled with one-hundred-twenty disciples. What follows is a dramatic demonstration of how God would use both men and women indiscriminately to spread the gospel.

We also know that Martha was not ultimately left in the kitchen. She too was honored by Jesus as a devoted disciple. In fact, it was to Martha that Jesus disclosed one of his greatest revelations.

> I am the resurrection and the life. Whoever believes in me, though he die, yet shall he live, and everyone who lives and believes in me shall never die. Do you believe this? (John 11:25-26)

Martha's response sets her apart as one of the first to recognize Jesus as more than just a rabbi, but God in the flesh.

> Yes, Lord; I believe that you are the Christ, the Son of God, who is coming into the world. (John 11:27)

THE SAMARITAN WOMAN

Over the years of missions work in various developing countries, we sponsored several women's conferences emphasizing women's new identity in Christ and how they reflect the image of God. I (Carol) frequently returned home questioning if our efforts even mattered or if anything could be done to change how womanhood was viewed in some of the places I taught. Overcome by discouragement, I found my own attitude becoming cynical that God could speak into the lives of women in such oppressive cultures. But when I read of the life-changing encounters women had with Jesus, my hope would be revived.

The Gospels record the transformation of severely marginalized women and the impact they had after a personal encounter with Jesus. Unlike other religious leaders of his day, Jesus spent time with women because he loved and valued them. He saw them as significant participants in his mission. In fact, the longest personal conversation recorded in the New Testament is between Jesus and a Samaritan woman. This is especially remarkable considering most Jews in that day wouldn't be caught dead speaking to a Samaritan, let alone a woman (John 4:9). When Jesus personally engaged this woman, he did so in violation of strict social, religious, and cultural norms.

The backstory for this unique encounter has Jesus and his disciples traveling from Judea through Samaria on their way to Galilee. Around noon they stopped at a well just outside a Samaritan village. Jesus stayed there to rest while the disciples went into the village to buy food. When a Samaritan woman came to the well, Jesus asked her for a drink of water.

The woman was astonished that a Jewish man would speak to her, much less receive water from her. His request opens the door to an intimate conversation in which Jesus reveals for the first time his true identity as the Christ or Messiah (John 4:4-42). Jesus also reveals without any hint of condemnation that he knows the woman's own life story, including her five past husbands and that she is currently living with a man outside of marriage.

This nameless, marginalized woman responds by returning to her village with the great news that she has just met the Messiah. Something must have been powerfully convincing about her testimony because the entire village rallied to come out and meet Jesus. This is a remarkable story of how one woman was used by God to change the destiny of her community. Despite the oppressive patriarchal culture of her day, her objectionable race, and low social status, this Samaritan woman was chosen to be the first evangelist recorded in the New Testament. Jesus didn't treat her with any tone of disrespect or judgment but rather deployed her to herald the gospel.

One African Christian ministry colleague especially stands out in my mind as an example of how women can have tremendous influence even in oppressive cultures. Her name is Blessed, which is very fitting to who she is. She runs an organization that works with women in remote African villages where it often feels as though one has stepped back in time. Women in these villages have little concept of self-care or self-respect. Traveling from village to village, she trains women through Bible studies and prayer groups to become spiritual leaders in their own communities. What she is doing in her country parallels the Samaritan woman's impact on her own community once she'd been transformed by her encounter with Jesus.

JESUS THE GOLD STANDARD

In his ministry, Jesus consistently refused to impose on women the customary prohibitions demanded by the extrabiblical religious traditions and secular culture of his day. It is easy to miss the significance of his encounters with women as recorded in the Gospels. They weren't just isolated incidents demonstrating Jesus's benevolent character but displayed a radical and permanent change in the religious and social order. Jesus inaugurated the arrival of the Kingdom of God and modeled the priorities of this new kingdom (Mark 1:15), reversing the curse that held men and women in bondage and revealing a new vision of life under his rulership (Galatians 3:13). He set an example for his followers to take up the baton of equality and fight for the rights of women as God's image-bearers.

Jesus is still calling, discipling, and empowering women to serve as his messengers today (John 20:17-18). He is certainly the gold standard in how women are to be esteemed. His example gives us hope that the church worldwide will continue to make progress toward the full emancipation of womanhood.

Chapter Twelve

Women Beyond the Cross

We've been tracking God's epic story beginning in the Garden of Eden, where we get a glimpse of God's original design. In creation, God formed Adam from the dust of the earth, then in response to Adam's aloneness, God formed the woman out of Adam's side. One became two so they could become one again in a marriage relationship marked by intimacy and equality. Together, they were commissioned to take dominion over the earth as co-regents.

We then saw how this position of authority was forfeited when the man and woman disobeyed God's one prohibition. Having lost their innocence, they turned their hearts away from God and began to look at each other in ways God never intended. The woman would now look to the man for her security and identity while the man would look to his wife as one to be ruled over and to serve him. Patriarchy became the new world order characterized by the strong dominating the weak and the weak serving the strong.

Nor was this Satanic world system only in relation to men and women. In every level of society, "might" became "right." The benevolent reign over the earth to which God had commissioned both man and woman became the oppressive, cruel rule of the strong and powerful over more vulnerable segments of society that lacked the means to defend themselves. For reasons already mentioned, the strong and powerful were generally male while women and children were typically the most vulnerable.

Satan would use this system of oppression to thwart the fruitfulness of the woman and her seed, for from the seed of the woman would come his greatest nemesis, the promised Messiah. We see the fruit of Satan's war on women chronicled in the Old Testament. Women are exploited and degraded but not without hope. God remained faithful to his image-bearers and their original relationship. His ultimate intention is to restore the full expression of women's dignity. God demonstrates this by choosing women to serve his purposes in remarkable ways far beyond the dictates of the patriarchal culture found in the Gentile world and the Jewish nation. These women exercised authority as judges and prophets over the nation of Israel. They served as God's mouthpiece and even lead armies to victory.

Then the long-awaited Messiah arrived on the scene to "set the oppressed free and to proclaim the year of the Lord's favor" (Luke 4:18, 19). Jesus announces the arrival of the Kingdom of God and invites women along with men to be his disciples and representatives of his new Kingdom. This Kingdom is a total reversal of worldly kingdoms where masters rule over slaves, the rich revile the poor, the religious despise sinners, and men subjugate women.

THE NEW RESTORES THE ORIGINAL

The death and resurrection of Jesus signals the beginning of the second creation narrative with Jesus as the second Adam conquering sin and death (I Corinthians 15:45-47). This signals a reversal of the judgment and curse of sin and the restoration of relationships back to God's original design. Men and women again become co-heirs and equal partners in expanding the newly arrived Kingdom. Renowned biblical scholar and historian N.T. Wright writes about the amazing results of the gospel in the emancipation of women.

> Imagine the thrill of equality brought about by baptism, the identical rite for Jew and Gentile, slave and free, male and female. And that's not all . . . If those in Christ are the true family of Abraham, which is the point of the whole story, then the manner of this identity and unity takes a quantum leap beyond the way in which first century Judaism construed them, bringing male and female together as surely as equally as Jew and Gentile.

The apostle Paul affirms this when he writes:

> For in Christ Jesus you are all sons of God through faith. For as many of you as were baptized into Christ have put on Christ. There is neither Jew nor Greek, there is neither slave nor free, there is neither male nor female, for you are all one in Christ Jesus. (Galatians 3:26-39)

As previously mentioned, even women are given the status of "sonship." Paul is not just talking about equal access to salvation but equal membership in the creation of a new family, a new humanity. This is verified by Paul's words to the Ephesian church.

> For he himself is our peace, who has made us both one (Jew and Gentile) and has broken down in his flesh the divided wall of hostility by abolishing the law of commandments and ordinance, that he might create in himself one new man in place of the two, so making peace. (Ephesians 2:14, 15)

What the apostle Paul is making clear here is that in Christ there is a new humanity that is not defined by race, gender, or social-economic classification. The barriers that had once separated men from women, slaves from freemen, Jews from Gentiles are all abolished in the new family of God. Patriarchy had dominated all of humanity with no recourse until the gospel brought us to the same place in redemptive history where there is no longer a privileged gender, race, or social class (Galatians 3:28).

Before the cross, the sign of circumcision distinguished Jewish males in a way which automatically privileged men. Paul now declares:

> In him also you [both men and women] were circumcised with a circumcision made without hands by putting off the body of the flesh, by the circumcision of Christ, having been buried with him in baptism, in which you were also raised with him through faith in the powerful working of God, who raised him from the dead. (Colossians 2:11, 12)

In Christ and through the revelation of the Gospel, everything has changed. It is the responsibility of the church and God's people to model this radical counter-cultural lifestyle. Promoting the equal standing of both men and women before God is a natural outflow of what Jesus accomplished through his life, death, and resurrection.

Misconstrued Hierarchical Logic

Before looking at how this "New Creation" plays out in the early church, let's look at how the narrative about womanhood is told by Christian leaders still holding to the old patriarchal view. In a podcast interview with a nationally known pastor who leads the charge in promoting patriarchy, he was asked: "Can a woman teach a mid-week class at church where men are present if she is given authority to do so by the elders so that she is functioning under the leadership of the church?" The question speaks for itself while the response speaks even louder. It went something like this.

> Absolutely not! A woman cannot function in any position of spiritual authority because the original sin had to do with her lack of submission to the man. The woman stepped out from under the man's authority, which was her assigned position by God prior to the fall. The man had been instructed by God not to eat of the Tree of the Knowledge of Good and Evil, and he subsequently gave that directive to the woman. She in turn acted in disobedience and without permission from the man. Man's first sin was to abdicate his position of authority over the woman, thereby leading to his disobedience and the Fall. Therefore a woman is not to teach or be

given authority over a man even by permission of the elders of the church.

Even having grown up in a Christian patriarchal culture, we had never heard this particular rationale articulated before. Our response was, "Say WHAT??????"

Unfortunately, knowing the nationwide influence of the pastor speaking gave us insight into what many pastors have been taught. This extrabiblical extrapolation is one of the pillars used to substantiate the patriarchal model. Although bemused by this interpretation, we see with greater clarity how the misconstrued hierarchical logic has permeated and infected the doctrinal landscape.

The same podcast posed another question equally perturbing. A male caller asked whether it was okay for a man to listen to Beth Moore's teaching. Beth Moore is a tremendously gifted Bible teacher highly regarded by even the most complementarian pastors, their caveat being that her audience should be limited to women. My (Carol) first thought was to wonder why an adult would find it necessary to seek approval to listen to Beth's teaching. The pastor responded with a conditional permission for the male caller to listen to Beth Moore "as long as you don't come under the authority of her teaching or be shepherded by her."

What a great opportunity was missed to acknowledge the amazing gift Beth has been to the church. Eric esteems her as an exceptionally gifted teacher in the body of Christ and has used her as a resource for his own sermons. This scrutinizing depreciation of female leaders and teachers by hardline proponents of male hierarchy can't possibly be what the writers of the New Testament intended.

Some pastors even question whether Beth Moore should be allowed to hold women's conferences on the basis that men aren't present to supervise her teaching and give it their approval. Some pastors oppose all women's ministries inside or outside the church because of their belief that women are prone to deception and need the direct supervision of men. Beth Moore's recent blog post entitled *A Letter to My Brothers* expresses her own dismay regarding the egregious, demeaning conduct she has endured from men for years as a female leader.

> As a woman leader . . . I accepted the peculiarities accompanying female leadership in a conservative Christian world because I chose to believe that, whether or not some of the actions and attitudes seemed ungodly to me, they were rooted in deep convictions . . . Then early October 2016 surfaced attitudes among some key Christian leaders that smacked of misogyny, objectification, and an astonishing disesteem of women . . . I came face to face with one of the most demoralizing realizations of my adult life. Scripture was not the reason for the colossal disregard and disrespect of women among many of these men. It was only used as the excuse. Sin was the reason; ungodliness.

Beth, you nailed it! You're our hero. And please, "Don't go home!" We need your voice to be heard more than ever.

Chapter Thirteen

Women in the Early Church

Following Jesus's resurrection and ascension, groups of Christians organized within the homes of believers. Those who could offer their home for meetings, many being women, assumed leadership roles and were considered influential within the movement. Several women are identified in those roles in the book of Acts and various apostolic epistles, as we will see later. In an article entitled *The Neglected History of Women in the Early Church* (*Christianity Today*, November 2017), the late Dr. Catherine Kroeger states:

> A number of prominent leaders, scholars, and benefactors of the early church were women, and despite neglect by many modern historians, the diligent researcher can still uncover a rich history.

She went on to say that one of the infamous secrets in Christianity is the enormous role that women played in the early church. It isn't surprising that the profile of women is more obscured than that given to men. Since sources of information stemming from the New Testament church have historically been written and interpreted by men, many have simply assumed it has always been a "man's church" with a "masculine feel."

Christianity emerged from patriarchal cultures that placed men in positions of authority in marriage, society, and government. While Judaism restricted the priesthood to males and denied theological training to women, this new movement offered women enhanced social and educational status. The "priesthood of every believer" taught by the apostles revolutionized the involvement of women and men. The historian Geoffrey Blainey wrote that women were more influential during the period of Jesus's brief ministry and into the first century of the church than they were in the next thousand years of Christianity.

History indicates that from early on women comprised a higher percentage than men within the Christian movement. Bishop Cyprian of Carthage once acknowledged that "Christian maidens" were so numerous it was difficult to find Christian husbands for all of them. One reason was the early church's practice of rescuing unwanted female infants from infanticide. Repudiating this practice, Christians adopted these unwanted baby girls into their households.

Also, women in high society often converted to Christianity before their husbands, who remained pagans in order to keep their economic and political status. Many of these women seized upon the opportunity to study the Bible as well as Hebrew and Greek. Their spiritual zeal led the way in social service and reform. This large female membership also resulted from the early church's informal and flexible organization that offered significant roles to women. There appeared to be no division between clergy and laity. Leadership was shared among male and female members according to their spiritual gifts and talents.

Even more important than the organization of the church was the way in which the gospel tradition, along with the writings of Paul, moved women beyond their previously limited involvement. Taboos and rituals in Judaism, such as those related to the menstrual cycle, previously limited women from even participating in public worship. The Jewish and pagan preference for male over female children also influenced large numbers of women converting to Christianity as well.

AFFIRMING WOMEN

Beyond the cross, we find the New Testament affirming women in unprecedented ways. In the book of Acts, women were a significant part of the Spirit's movement. Even before the church was officially born on the day of Pentecost, we see women sharing in the community life of the church.

> All these with one accord were devoting themselves to prayer, together with the women and Mary, the mother of Jesus, and his brothers. (Acts 1:14)

In the very next chapter, the apostle Peter explains the coming of the Holy Spirit on the Day of Pentecost by quoting from Joel 2:28-29.

> "In the last days it shall be," God declares, "that I will pour out my Spirit on all flesh, and your sons and your daughters shall prophesy, and your young men shall see visions, and your old men shall dream dreams; even on my male servants and female servants in those days I will pour out my Spirit, and they shall prophesy." (Acts 2:17, 18)

The prophet Joel, the apostle Peter, and the Holy Spirit all bore witness to the reality that not just sons but daughters, both men and women, were recognized as having spiritual gifts and were permitted to prophesy in the church (1 Corinthians 11:5). Prophetic words carried spiritual authority as described in 1 Corinthians 14:3-4.

> But one who prophesies speaks to men for edification and exhortation and consolation. One who speaks in a tongue edifies himself; but one who prophesies edifies the church.

It goes without saying that prophetic words included both an encouraging and instructional component, indicating that women as well as men were given authority in the church. Women would obviously be included in the description of early church worship services found in 1 Corinthians 14:26.

> What then shall we say, brothers and sisters? When you come together, each one has a hymn, a word of instruction, a revelation, a tongue, or an interpretation. Let all things be done for building up.

The Power of Everyone

As pastors for over three decades, we (Eric and Carol) have been significantly involved behind the scenes in preparing for Sunday services week in and week out. Many moving parts are involved in meeting the expectations of those who have come for worship. If you were to ask those attending what they liked most, you would hear a variety of responses. "The worship music was the best ever." "The pastor crushed it with his message." "Communion was especially meaningful."

If you asked a first century Christian the same question, you'd get a totally different response. The apostle Paul lets us know what he valued most when God's people gathered.

> How is it then, brethren? When you come together, every one of you has a psalm, a doctrine, a tongue, a revelation, an interpretation. Let all things be done unto edifying. (1 Corinthians 14:26)

What Paul describes here is what we like to refer to as "The Power of Everyone." In the early church, every believer was invited to participate in the service, and their contributions were evidence of God's presence in their midst. In fact, Paul states in the prior verse that when everyone is using their gifts to glorify God, unbelievers will "fall down and worship God, exclaiming 'God is really among you'" (v. 25).

Obviously the "everyone" Paul mentions here includes both men and women because he directs his instructions in verse 26 to "brothers and sisters." There is no injunction against women speaking and teaching. It is evident that Paul is not restricting participation in public worship services based on gender. Nothing in this chapter prohibits women from participating in any aspect of public worship.

The first question that may come to mind is how this dynamic and spontaneous interaction is possible. Most often when the early church gathered, it was in homes much like our small groups today. In those settings, more people had the opportunity to do what Paul describes, speaking words of inspiration and encouragement. These are the "prophetic" communications Paul references with both men and women sharing God's word. We can remember experiencing this same dynamic during our early "Jesus People" days while meeting in house churches. If anyone had a song, a scripture or an insight to share, there was an opportunity in the gatherings to do just that.

After exhorting "everyone" to participate, Paul concludes by making a profoundly important statement: "all of these must be done for the strengthening of the church" (1 Corinthians 14:26). There is no doubt about what Paul is saying here, who he is saying it to, and why it is so important. He is speaking emphatically about one of the most important elements for building up the body of Christ, the church.

While small group gatherings are still a priority in many churches, the logistics of how people gather for core worship services today has greatly changed. In many modern-day church services, participants basically come to watch a skilled group of professionals conduct the service. We understand that in a large church gathering not everyone can have a speaking part. At the same time, the truth about the power of "everyone" hasn't changed.

> From him the whole body, joined and held together by EVERY supporting ligament, grow and builds itself up in love, as EACH PART DOES ITS WORK. (Ephesians 4:16)

According to the pattern of the New Testament, the strengthening of the church is dependent upon the vital contribution of both men and women sharing their spiritual gifts, Shouldn't it then be the job of church leadership to give serious consideration to how the "everyone" principle can be more effectively incorporated back into the culture of the church as we see taught in these passages?

NOT WITHOUT CONFLICT

In Acts 16, we are introduced to Lydia, a businesswoman who became a convert under Paul's teaching. She immediately opened her home to form the nucleus of the first church in Europe (Acts 16:15, 40). Lydia and women like her were vital players at the forefront of the expanding Christian mission. It is to the church in Philippi that Paul later exhorts two women leaders to resolve a conflict.

> I entreat Euodia and I entreat Syntyche to agree in the Lord. Yes, I ask you also, true companion, help these women who have labored side by side with me in the gospel together with Clement and the rest of my fellow workers, whose names are in the book of life. (Philippians 4:2-3)

This was no small quarrel. It involved two significant church leaders Paul describes as laboring side by side with him. Lydia along with these two women played a significant role in the leadership and development of the church at Philippi.

A Wife-Husband Team

The leadership team of Priscilla and Aquila are mentioned six times in the New Testament. Of those six references, Priscilla is listed before her husband four times. This priority of listing Priscilla before Aquila cannot be accidental. Many scholars understand this to signify Priscilla as having the primary role in their ministry together. A comparable example would be how "Barnabas and Paul" are listed as ministry partners in Acts 11:25; 12:25; 13:2, 7. But as Paul begins taking a more prominent role than Barnabas, their names are reversed to "Paul and Barnabas" (Acts 13:13, 34).

In Acts 18:24-26, the couple take on a new role that emphasizes even more clearly Priscilla's spiritual leadership and the teaching role she played.

> Now a Jew named Apollos, a native of Alexandria, came to Ephesus. He was an eloquent man, competent in the Scriptures. He had been instructed in the way of the Lord. And being fervent in spirit, he spoke and taught accurately the things concerning Jesus, though he knew only the baptism of John. He began to speak boldly in the synagogue, but when Priscilla and Aquila heard him, they took him and explained to him the way of God more accurately.

Apollos was a visiting minister who had come to preach and teach in the Ephesian church. After hearing his teaching, Priscilla and Aquilla recognized that his theological understanding was incomplete, so they took him aside to explain "the way of God more accurately." The radically egalitarian nature of early Christian communities is clearly evidenced here by the fact that a woman and her husband are correcting the theology of an up-and-coming apostle. No one else is mentioned as instructing this prominent visiting minister. Since this function would typically be the role of proven leaders, the public acknowledgment of Priscilla's prominent role along with her husband leaves little doubt she was a well-known minister and leader in Ephesus.

Many years later, the apostle Paul acknowledges Priscilla and Aquila, who are now leaders in the church in Rome.

> Greet Prisca [Priscilla] and Aquila, my fellow workers in Christ Jesus, who risked their necks for my life, to whom not only I give thanks but all the churches of the Gentiles give thanks as well. Greet also the church in their house. (Romans 16:3-5)

The phrase "the church in their house" is an indication of Priscilla and Aquila's dual role as pastors. Before Christianity became a legal religion in the year 313, congregations couldn't legally own property, so they met in homes. Paul further describes Priscilla and Aquila as his "fellow workers". This term, *sunergos* in Greek, is the same term Paul also used for Titus (2 Corinthians 8:23) and Timothy (Romans 16:21), who were pastors, teachers, and elders.

In addition to Paul's gratitude for their sacrifice, "all the churches of the Gentiles give thanks as well." This last statement makes clear that Priscilla and Aquila weren't just local church pastors but a dynamic leadership team who ministered throughout Asia. How would this level of influence have ever been possible had Priscilla been required to "be silent" and live out the traditional role expected of woman of that time and culture?

Prophetic Quartet

When viewed in the light of 1 Corinthians 11:4-5 where the church is instructed on how men and women are to conduct themselves when prophesying, clearly women exercised prophetic gifts in the early church. In Acts 21:9, we learn that Philip the Evangelist, one of the seven first deacons chosen to help the apostles (Acts 6) "had four unmarried daughters who prophesied." The ancient church historian Eusebius of Caesarea makes clear that Philip's four daughters held a prominent position in the early church (Ecclesiastical History 3.37.1), and they appear to have exercised their prophetic gifts freely within the church as a fulfillment of Joel's prophecy. Dr. F. F. Bruce adds:

> The daughters [of Philip] were highly esteemed as informants on persons and events belonging to the early years of Judean Christianity. There is reason to believe that the information which Philip and his daughters were able to give about these things was highly prized by Luke, who made use of the information in the composition of his twofold work—not only during the few days which he spent at Caesarea now, but also during the two years

during which Paul was kept in custody there. (*Commentary on the Book of the Acts*, p. 424)

A Trusted Minister

Along with Priscilla and Aquila, Paul also mentions Phoebe when he writes to the church in Rome, telling them that she is a minister of the church at Cenchreae.

> I commend to you our sister Phoebe, a deacon of the church in Cenchreae. I ask you to receive her in the Lord in a way worthy of his people and to give her any help she may need from you, for she has been the benefactor of many people, including me. (Romans 16:1-2)

Paul refers to Phoebe as both sister and deacon, or *diakonos*. In using the term *diakonos*, Paul is describing Phoebe with the same word he used to describe himself, Apollos, Tychicus, Epaphras, and Timothy. Paul also refers to Phoebe as a patron, or benefactor, of many, including himself. This indicates that Phoebe like Lydia (Acts 16) was an independently wealthy woman.

Unfortunately, in many English translations the word *diakonos* has been translated servant instead of deacon. But Phoebe couldn't have been a servant in the usual sense of that word. As a wealthy woman, she would have had servants of her own. Patronage was a part of the social system of the first century Greco-Roman world, so Phoebe would have had substantial economic and political influence. Furthermore, it is widely accepted that Phoebe travelled from Cenchrea, a port town of Corinth, and very likely hand-delivered Paul's letter to the Christians in Rome. She was clearly a trusted minister on whom Paul relied and commended to the church at large.

In summation, when understood correctly Paul's statements about women in his epistles encourage the ministry of godly and gifted women. They especially shouldn't discourage women, young or old, from ministering as messengers of Jesus Christ with whatever talent or gift they have been given. Paul loved and valued his female co-workers, and there is no evidence that he silenced or limited these women.

Chapter Fourteen

The Church Gets Off Track

In reviewing the progression of redemptive history since the time of the early church, we can see the ebb and flow of the church's advancement and decline. In the first century we witnessed a radical advancement of the gospel. Both men and women exercised spiritual gifts and abilities as the Holy Spirit determined. The lists of spiritual gifts we find in Romans 12:3-8, 1 Corinthians 12:4-11, Ephesians 4:7-13, and 1 Peter 4:10 offer no indication that gender played a factor in their distribution. The Holy Spirit showed no partiality based on race, gender, or social status (Acts 10:34-35) as the gospel spread throughout the known world.

At the point when the church evolved into a government supported and imposed religion, it became a source of power, wealth, and fame. As the church's temporal power and influence grew, its vitality was lost along with the kingdom culture modeled by Jesus and taught in the early church. The church lost its clear gospel message of servanthood and impartiality. The priesthood of the believer (1 Peter 2:5, 9), which gave everyone the privilege to relate to God directly, was overtaken by the control of organized religion. Especially after the Emperor Constantine instituted Christianity as the Roman empire's official religion.

As the church became more political and institutionalized, the influential public involvement of women diminished while men increasingly held positions of power over the people. By the Middle Ages, much of orthodox faith was lost to a perversion of the gospel and a stranglehold by male ecclesiastic structure. We know from church history that the hard-won equality of women at the cross lost ground to exclusively male leadership.

Extending roughly from 150-500 AD, the patristic era is considered to be even harsher than the Middle Ages in attributing restrictive roles to women, hence the expression "patriarchy." You can hear a satanic whisper in each of the following degrading statements coming from some of the brightest and influential theologians and church fathers.

CLEMENT OF ALEXANDRIA
THEOLOGIAN AND CHURCH FATHER, 150-215

> His beard then is the badge of a man . . . is the symbol of the stronger nature. By God's decree, hairiness is one of man's conspicuous qualities . . . Whatever smoothness or softness there was in him God took from him when he fashioned the delicate Eve from his side to be the receptacle of his seed, his helpmate both in procreation and in the management of the home . . . therefore, the male is hairier and more warm-blooded than the female; the uncastrated than the castrated;

the mature than the immature. Thus, it is a sacrilege to trifle with the symbol of manhood.

ORIGEN
THEOLOGIAN AND GREEK FATHER, 2ND-3RD CENTURIES

From *Fragments on 1 Corinthians*: Men should not sit and listen to a woman . . . even if she says admirable things, or even saintly things, that is, of little consequence, since it came from the mouth of a woman.

TERTULLIAN
THE FATHER OF LATIN CHRISTIANITY, 155-245

From *De Cultu Feminarium* (*On the Apparel of Women*, chapter 1: Woman is a Temple Built Over a Sewer):

Do you not know that you are (each) an Eve? The sentence of God on this sex of yours lives in this age: the guilt must of necessity live too. You are the devil's gateway: you are the unsealer of that (forbidden) tree: you are the first deserter of the divine law: you are she who persuaded him whom the devil was not valiant enough to attack. You destroyed so easily God's image, man. On account of your desert—that is, death—even the Son of God had to die. And do you think about adorning yourself over and above your tunics of skins?

CHRYSOSTOM
ARCHBISHOP OF CONSTANTINOPLE, DOCTOR OF THE CHURCH, FOURTH CENTURY

From *Homily 9 on First Timothy:* The [female] sex is weak and fickle.

From *The Kind of Women Who Ought to Be Taken as Wives*: God maintained the order of each sex by dividing the business of life into two parts, and assigned the more necessary and beneficial aspects to the man and the less important, inferior matter to the woman.

Cited in *Cooper-White 2012:72:* Among all the savage beasts none is found to be so harmful as woman . . . The whole of her body is nothing less than phlegm, blood, bile, and the fluid of digested food . . . If you consider what is stored up behind those lovely eyes, the angle of the nose, the mouth and the cheeks you will agree that the well-proportioned body is only a whitened sepulcher.

AUGUSTINE
BISHOP OF HIPPO, DOCTOR OF THE CHURCH AND LATIN FATHER, 354-430

From *De Genesi ad literam* (*The Literal Meaning of Genesis*) 9.5.9: I don't see what sort of help woman was created to provide man with, if one excludes procreation. If woman is not given to man for help in bearing children, for what help could she be? To till the earth together? If help were needed for that, man would have been a better help for man. The same goes for comfort in solitude.

How much more pleasure is it for life and conversation when two friends live together than when a man and a woman cohabitate?

From *Letter to Laetus* (Letter 243.10): Watch out that she does not twist and turn you for the worse. What is the difference whether it is in a wife or a mother, it is still Eve the temptress that we must beware of in any woman.

These profoundly misogynistic declarations bear witness against the ugliness of patriarchy. Such a depreciation of women is an insult of their Maker and defames half the image of God.

MARCELLA OF AVENTINE HILL

Regardless of these pervasive patriarchal attitudes, in the late fourth century, various Roman women studied with Saint Jerome, known for his translation of the Bible from Greek and Hebrew into Latin. As documented in his correspondence, these women showed great scholarship. Marcella was one such outstanding scholar to whom Jerome would often refer church elders for the resolution of hermeneutical problems. A young widow, Marcella pledged herself to celibacy rather than remarrying, devoting her life to God and the study of the Bible.

Marcella owned a palace on Aventine Hill that became a center of Christian activity. She turned her palace into a refuge for other upper-class women wishing to devote their lives to Christianity. Sadly, when the Goths invaded Rome in 410 AD, they ransacked the Aventine Hill palace, where she was brutalized and died of her injuries shortly after. To console her beloved students after her death, Saint Jerome wrote a tribute to her life. In it he wrote the following about his relationship with Marcella.

> How much virtue and intellect, how much holiness and purity I found in her I am afraid to say, both least I may exceed the bounds of men's belief and least I increase your sorrow by reminding you of the blessings you have lost. This only will I say, that whatever I had gathered together by long study and by constant meditation made part of my nature she tasted, she learned and made her own.

The reputation of Marcella's life and Christian refuge prompted the formation of several other similar groups in Rome, the beginning of the Roman monastic movement.

Records from the Ecumenical Council's six centuries of church history indicate that the church did continue to endorse the ordained diaconate of women. The Council of Chalcedon in 451 AD confirmed the ordination of women with the specification that they needed to be forty years of age or older. Women, particularly of aristocratic status, continued to study the Scriptures. With the establishment of Christian monasticism, other influential roles became available to women.

From the fifth century onward, Christian convents provided an alternative for some women to the path of marriage and child-rearing. This allowed them to acquire literacy and learning and to play a more active religious role. While non-aristocratic women were largely excluded from political and mercantile life in the Middle Ages, leading church women were an exception. Medieval abbesses and female superiors of monastic houses were powerful figures whose influence could rival that of male bishops and abbots.

A Two-Edged Sword

With the beginning of the Protestant reformation in the sixteenth century, we see the church coming back to life. Many precious truths of the gospel were recovered with renewed fervency and accuracy. As chains of institutionalism, ignorance, and ecclesiastical control were broken, the renewal of the church began to spread across Europe. We thank God that through the Reformation doctrines like the following five *Solas* were restored to the church.

- *Sola Gratia* – Grace Alone
- *Sola Fide* – Faith Alone
- *Solus Christus* – Christ Alone
- *Sola Scriptura* – Scripture Alone
- *Soli Deo Gloria* – Glory of God Alone

But the Reformation proved to be a two-edged sword when it came to women's involvement in ministry. While believers were now given the opportunity to read and study the Scriptures for themselves, making the priesthood of all believers a reality again, women's equality was not only opposed but opportunities for devoting oneself to biblical studies were no longer available. Where the Reformation took control, convents were shut down, essentially closing off the only option of a full-time religious role for women as well as one that had offered them a life in academic study.

Women now had only the option of marriage and domestic life. Although they found salvation by faith, the new freedom discovered in Christ was incomplete. They were once again denied an opportunity for theological training and positions in ministry. Nor were women the only ones experiencing discrimination, Jews were hated, and slavery continued to be promoted. While the Reformation had brought about tremendous change in important areas of theology, the reformers had missed important truths spoken by the apostle Paul.

> There is neither Jew nor Gentile, neither slave nor free, nor is there male and female, for you are all one in Christ Jesus. (Galatians 3:28)

The prejudice against women promoted by the reformers is profoundly disturbing. The following quotes from church fathers expose their ignorance and shameful attitudes.

Martin Luther
German Priest, Theologian, and Protestant Reformer
1483-1546

From *Commentary on Genesis*, Chapter 2, Part V, 27b: For woman seems to be a creature somewhat different from man, in that she has dissimilar members, a varied form and a mind weaker than man. Although Eve was a most excellent and beautiful creature, like unto Adam in reference to the image of

God, that is with respect to righteousness, wisdom and salvation, yet she was a woman. For as the sun is more glorious than the moon, though the moon is a most glorious body, so woman, though she was a most beautiful work of God, yet she did not equal the glory of the male creature.

The word and works of God is quite clear, that women were made either to be wives or prostitutes.

JOHN CALVIN
FRENCH THEOLOGIAN, PASTOR AND PROTESTANT REFORMER
1509-1564

From *Commentary on the Gospel of John* (John 20) on the first post-resurrection appearance of Jesus to women rather than to men: I consider this was done by way of reproach, because they [the men] had been so tardy and sluggish to believe. And indeed, they deserve not only to have women for their teachers, but even oxen and asses . . . Yet it pleased the Lord, by means of those weak and contemptible vessels, to give display of his power.

From *Commentary on 1 Corinthians 11*: On this account, all women are born that they may acknowledge themselves as inferior in consequence to the superiority of the male sex.

Reformed theology's support of patriarchy finds its roots in these unbiblical attitudes and prejudices. It is no wonder that the main current of Christianity produced a steady diet of misogyny in the church for so many decades. Their influence is sadly still felt in the church today.

Chapter Fifteen

The Early Women's Movement

In *A Very Short History of the World*, Geoffrey Blainey wrote that in removing the institution of the convent, the Reformation initially reduced the involvement of women in the church since convents had been places where women could be involved and achieve influence. In comparison to the recorded writings of women during the medieval period, only a few Protestant women seemed apt or interested in articulating their theological views. Even fewer were in a position to enter the public dominion of theological discourse.

However, the Protestant belief that all people should be able to read the Bible led to an increase in female literacy as a result of the opening of new schools and the introduction in 1717 of compulsory education for boys and girls. While they have received little recognition, a significant part of the Reformation was championed by women working alongside men. Unfortunately, those women were largely airbrushed out of history, their contributions forgotten, their voices silenced.

In his book *Mrs. Luther and Her Sisters*, British historian Derek Wilson sets the record straight as to how women were crucial to the Reformation. From Catharina Luther and English martyr Anne Askew to Queen Elizabeth I and onwards out into Europe, Wilson's book uncovers the influence that Christian women brought to the renewal of the church. Just as the women who partnered with Jesus and Paul in the New Testament helped shape biblical history, so the women of the Reformation help shape the future of the church.

While discrimination of women fostered by patriarchy remained a stronghold in the church, courageous Christian women began to impact the culture outside the church. Their involvement in social reform encompassed assisting the poor, opposing child labor laws, supporting the abolition of slavery, and women's suffrage. These were all crucial moral and spiritual turning points. Regrettably, many Christian leaders aligned themselves on the wrong side of history in their opposition and support of male primacy.

FLORENCE NIGHTINGALE

In the seventeenth through nineteenth centuries, Christian women went on to play a central role in the developing and managing of many of the modern world's education and health care systems. Notable women like Florence Nightingale assisted with the development of modern nursing. Her desire to serve in the ministry of the church had been denied, and she is quoted as saying:

I would have given my church my head, my hand, my heart. She would not have them. She did not know what to do with them. She told me to go back and do crochet in my mother's drawing room; or if I was tired of that to marry and look well at the head of my husband's table . . . "You may go to the Sunday School if you like it," she said. But she gave me no training even for that. She gave me neither work to do for her nor education for it.

Phoebe Palmer

Advancement in ministry for women began to take shape in the 1800s. In 1837, Phoebe Palmer, a Methodist evangelist and writer, began leading the Tuesday Meeting for the Promotion of Holiness. At first only women attended these meetings, but eventually Methodist bishops and other clergy members also began to attend. She is considered one of the founders of the Holiness movement within Methodist Christianity.

William and Catherine Booth

In 1859, Palmer published *The Promise of the Father*, in which she argued in favor of women in ministry. This would later influence the founders of the Salvation Army, William and Catherine Booth. William Booth insisted on gender equality, writing in 1908:

> Every office and soldier should insist upon the truth that woman is as important, as valuable, as capable, and as necessary to the progress and happiness of the world as man.

Booth is also noted for the famous quote: "My best men are women." Women have been prominent in leadership positions throughout the history of the Salvation Army. In 1934, Evangeline Booth was elected as its first female general, a worldwide position of leadership.

Many Christian women were instrumental in the movement for women's suffrage, which achieved its first successes in Britain's Australasian colonies at the close of the nineteenth century. It then spread across the democratic world. In the United States, the Quaker sisters were early advocates of abolitionism and women's rights.

Susan B. Anthony

We must applaud and celebrate the devotion and sacrifice of women down through history. But in order to do that, their stories need to be heard. The influence on American history of one woman in particular aroused a sleeping world regarding the unjust depreciation and disregard of women. Susan B. Anthony was an American social reformer and women's rights activist who played a pivotal role in both the abolition of slavery and the woman's suffrage movement.

Anthony was an extremely courageous pioneer and trailblazer for the right of all people to be equal in the eyes of God. To say that she was "no shrinking violet" is an understatement. When she first began campaigning for women's rights, she was harshly ridiculed and accused of trying to destroy the institution of marriage. But public perception of her changed radically during her lifetime, and her eightieth birthday was celebrated in the White House at the invitation of President William McKinley. She became the first female citizen to be depicted on U.S. coinage when her portrait appeared on the 1979-dollar coin.

Susan B. Anthony was instrumental in winning women the right to vote. She presented Congress with an amendment that became known colloquially as the Susan B. Anthony Amendment. It was later ratified as the Nineteenth Amendment of the Constitution in 1920. It is hard for us to comprehend today that in a democracy like the United States of America women were denied voting rights up until 1920, just one hundred years ago!

We all know about how the Women's Suffrage Movement ended with the passing of the Nineteenth Amendment to the Constitution in 1920. But what most people don't know is that these efforts began in 1848. That's right, it took seventy-two years for women to win the right to vote because of the profoundly misogynistic attitude accepted and even promoted by society, culture, and the church. Many in the church advocated against women as equal to men for years, using the misinterpretation of Scripture for their support.

It's interesting to note that while Susan B. Anthony witnessed the abolition of slavery in her lifetime, she didn't live to see her other lifelong dream fulfilled. She died in 1906 at the age of eighty-six—fourteen years before a woman's right to vote became a reality. Today women are no longer struggling for the right to vote. But there is more to be achieved in God's redemptive plan for his daughters. While the abolition of slavery was achieved, ugly prejudice in the hearts of men is still a battle needing to be won. Likewise, discrimination and opposition toward women remains in hearts still controlled by patriarchy. The church is the only place on earth where all people can find equal standing, a place where the discrimination of social status, gender, and race can and must be opposed.

In recent decades, the ordination of women in Protestant churches is on the rise. As of 1996, over half of American Protestant denominations ordain women, though most restrict official positions a woman can hold. For instance, some ordain women for the military, hospital chaplaincy, or missions work but prohibit them from serving in congregational roles.

Still, one-third to one half of all seminary students today are female. With this renewed hunger and desire in women to study Scripture and serve Jesus well, how is the church going to respond? Will the church continue to deny women a role in teaching and leading? Or will such women be forced into the secular workplace to use their God-given gifts?

A Call to All Women

When one reads the stories of courageous pioneering women like Marcella, Phoebe Palmer, Catherine Booth, and Suzanne D. Anthony, hope is rekindled that women can have significant influence in shaping church culture. We're not simply talking about a handful of female super-stars like notable women in the limelight today. We're talking about the "everyday" women who represent the body of Christ, equally called and chosen to be on the front lines advancing the Kingdom of God. Everywhere we look, God is issuing a renewed call for women to begin serving in vital leadership positions.

We need to be reminded that God doesn't call the qualified. Rather, he qualifies the called, whether they be male or female, as seen in the lives of men and women he chose to use throughout redemptive history. The apostle Paul put it this way:

> Brothers and sisters, think of what you were when you were called. Not many of you were wise by human standards; not many were influential; not many were of noble birth. But God chose the foolish things of the world to shame the wise; God chose the weak things of the world to shame the strong; God chose the lowly things of this world and the despised things and the thing that are not to nullify things that are, so tht no one may boast before him. (1 Corinthians 1:26-30)

There is no greater witness to this principle of how God's kingdom works than his prerogative to use women, who in this world's system of patriarchy are disregarded and denigrated, to represent him and speak on his behalf.

In speaking of the New Covenant, Jesus once made the analogy that new wine must be poured into new wineskins (Mark 2:22) because old wineskins were too brittle to contain the fermenting new wine and would burst, ruining both the wineskins and new wine. What Jesus was expressing here was that the Old Covenant could not contain the liberating new gospel Jesus had come to proclaim. Our hope and prayer is that the church will develop "new wineskins" of ministry opportunities that are flexible and receptive to the female leaders God is raising up.

Of course for this to happen, the old, dry, and inflexible wineskin of patriarchy must be replaced with a new wineskin of equal respect for women. We believe a re-examination of Scripture gives us that new wineskin. We need to open our eyes to the historical record of how God has significantly used women to shape the birth and rebirth of the church.

Until recently, women have not been encouraged to pursue careers in pastoral ministry or given opportunities for leadership development in the church. The church must take responsibility for failing to offer women viable pathways to develop and employ their leadership gifts in local church ministry. There is no question that a gifted woman brings a unique viewpoint that is missed when men do all the teaching and leading. There is something particularly impressive and powerful to hear a woman who is a dynamic communicator and Bible teacher. Is it because we are just surprised that a woman could be that capable?

A Liberating Heritage

One such gifted woman had an unforgettable impact on me (Carol) when I was attending an Exponential Conference for church planters and leaders. Against the entire line-up of men on the program, there was only one female speaker, an officer in the Salvation Army named Danielle Strickland. Along with being an outstanding spiritual leader, she was equally commanding in her presentation. She came across powerfully feminine yet spoke with a freedom and confidence devoid of any sense of intimidation despite addressing an audience primarily made up of men. After she spoke, several of the male pastors attending accompanying me agreed she was by far the most dynamic speaker in the entire conference.

As mentioned earlier, the Salvation Army was co-founded by Catherine Booth with her husband. What a liberating heritage they left behind. I could only thank God that Danielle Strickland had come from such an egalitarian tradition that allowed women to participate in leadership ministries of the church. But I was also left wondering how many other women with the potential to be teachers and leaders have been denied that opportunity.

For several years, I had the special privilege of teaching Sunday school classes attended by both men and women. The priesthood of the believer was a favorite topic highlighting the equal access of men and women in relating to God. Unlike the restrictive priesthood in the Old Testament, there was no gender requirement when ministering to God in worship or representing God's people in intercession. It is hard to imagine that God, who has no problem with women coming boldly into his presence (Hebrew 4:16), would disavow women from ministering on his behalf to men or women.

Helping men and women discover their gifts during our church's membership labs was also a privilege I enjoyed. These classes focused on understanding each believer's unique design for fulfilling God's purpose. Though I taught this class for over twenty years, I never lost the thrill of watching self-discovery compel people to greater involvement and fulfillment in our church and God's kingdom.

Part of my job was also to help each new member connect with a ministry leader within our church and get plugged into a ministry that could use their gifts. My observation was that just as many women as men were scoring high in leadership, and the women were often more willing to get actively involved. But sadly, there were also many prohibitions placed on the women as to available roles they could fill, a clear contradiction to me with how the Bible teaches that the body of Christ should properly function.

THE GLORY OF WOMANHOOD?

As the senior pastor's wife, I was also given a few opportunities to speak on Sunday morning. I always felt awkward and less effective than in the classroom. A contributing factor was an assumption that I had to project an unassuming, self-effacing demeanor that made clear I was just "sharing" and not usurping anyone's authority.

Then in 2004, I was given the opportunity to participate in a pastor's conference in West Africa. It was there I felt the freedom to teach God's word without self-censorship. Looking back over the twenty years of my involvement in missions, I thank God for the privilege of speaking to thousands of pastors and their wives in Africa, Latin America, North America, and elsewhere.

Still, I was always careful to give deference to male authority, assuring the pastors I had my husband's permission to be speaking at the conference and was doing so under his authority. On one mission trip, I was invited by an Anglican bishop to speak at his church. He wanted me to challenge the women of his congregation to serve more diligently. He thought the women would be inspired by hearing a woman speak in the Sunday morning service. I felt honored and accepted his invitation.

That morning I spoke on the glory of womanhood, sharing how women were indispensable to the church if "she" was ever to become the glorious bride of Christ. Many of the women there were from poverty-stricken backgrounds with lives of hard labor in a particularly harsh patriarchal society. As I looked at their tired faces, I realized I was exhorting these overworked, undervalued women to "do more" when the real problem was that their culture, male family members, and church did not permit them to "be more." There was something very wrong with this picture where women comprised most of the congregation and its workforce but without representation in leadership.

There is a sadness I feel reflecting on that experience and the realization that this same picture exists within the North American church as well as other historically Christian nations. While equal opportunities for women are now available in every other professional field, the door is closed to many women with gifts and abilities needed by the church.

Still, change is taking place, and women need to be ready to step up. Those women with leadership gifts need to consider how to be equipped for involvement as doors do open up. All Christian women need to ask how they can more fully reflect God's image and identity.

We are now living beyond the cross and under new rulership in Jesus's Kingdom. As women, we need a clearer vision of how the Lordship of Christ is to be honored in our life. We should also know when his Lordship is being compromised. Perhaps when a woman looks to a man for permission as opposed to confidently joining him as a partner in doing God's will? Or when a woman looks to a man for her identity and security versus for comradery and mutuality? A woman's victory must first be won within her own heart by dethroning the idolatry of men and regaining her equal standing alongside them.

Part III:

Opening Doors Closed to Women

"For it is improper for a woman to speak in an assembly . . . even if she says . . . saintly things, that is of little consequence, since they come from the mouth of a woman."

—Origen

"Even on my servants, both men and women, I will pour out my Spirit in those days and they will prophesy."

—God

Chapter Sixteen

The Eye of the Beholder

We all have ideological blind spots, or *scotomas*, that obscure our vision of reality. In the Greek, a scotoma is "a partially blocked alteration in one's field of vision which diminishes one's visual acuity."

The apostle Paul described our lack of clear vision when he said, "For now we see in a mirror dimly" (1 Corinthians 13:12). For many years, my (Eric) vision for women in leadership could only be seen "dimly." It was as if I'd been wearing blinders like those used by horse trainers. Also called blinkers or pacifiers, these blinders are used to keep horses focused and undistracted. Such was the effect on me by the persistent indoctrination of the patriarchal-complementarian worldview.

One of the most unsettling parts about the research Carol and I have done in tracking the story of womanhood since creation was discovering how much we didn't know and how much of what we thought we knew was incorrect. While we'd assumed what we'd been taught was the "narrow way that leads to life" (Matthew 7:14), we came to realize it was simply the "narrow-minded way that leads to ignorance." As we took a deeper look into history, tradition, and the Scriptures, we found ourselves dissatisfied with the standard answers to why the church has restricted the participation of women in leadership.

I (Eric) had been a committed complementarian throughout my forty-five years in ministry. With support of my own sinful nature and the encouragement of the prevailing evangelical position, I made the decision to tacitly support many of the traditional restrictions against women in church leadership. In retrospect, I now regret allowing my fear and uncertainty to minimize a very serious problem and marginalize qualified women from participating in the leadership of church life. I also recognize that a large part of my motivation was the fear of judgment, criticism, and rejection from my complementarian brothers.

My complementarian stance was strengthened by listening to men preaching sermons against women in leadership using 1 Corinthians 14:34 and 1 Timothy 2:12. These two verses are considered by complementarians "unshakable pillars" supporting male hierarchy in the church, also referred to as "prohibitive texts" or "clobber verses." At first glance, these passages seem straightforward, biblical, and incontrovertible. In fact, some have gone so far as to claim this issue as a quick litmus test of whether a church teaches the Bible or not. Just ask if they would allow a woman to occupy a significant position of leadership. If they say yes, then you know they don't care about the authority of Scripture.

These critics will also say that egalitarian Christians are following the way of world, not the Word of God. They are conforming to culture, not to Christ. They are surrendering to social pressure, not to scriptural teaching. I am very aware that my own prayerfully developed convictions on this topic are antithetical to many good friends within our Christian ministry circles.

That said, I have personally chosen to stop turning a blind eye to this theological elephant in the room. There is something wrong with mixing patriarchy with the New Covenant. In Part III of this book, we will look at some of the most critical passages used to support the claim that patriarchy is still God's design for moving God's Kingdom forward.

Misleading Mistranslations

In today's evangelical church, along with other denominations including Catholic and Orthodox, men are the ones teaching the Bible and doctrine, and a dogmatic part of their preaching is to say that women can't do the same. We shouldn't be surprised that this imbalance of perspectives has contributed to a biased lens through which believers read Scripture. Not only does this bias create blinders when reading and studying Scripture, but even some Bible translations have a distinct gender prejudice.

Christians who are serious about studying the Bible need to be aware of how easy it is for translators to incorporate their own ideas into the translation process. It is no secret that some Bible translators have been willing to interpret certain passages to reflect their convictions even if the interpretation can't be justified by the text itself.

Let's begin with an example that takes us back to the beginnings of biblical history. Specifically, Genesis 3:16, where the consequences of the Fall for the woman are addressed. For the sake of comparison, let's look first at this verse in the *New International Version* (NIV), where an accurate formal translation describes: "Your desire (*teshuqah*) will be for your husband, and he will rule over you."

Before the Fall, Adam and Eve—husband and wife—were equal in every way. But as we have previously discussed, when sin entered the world one consequence was that men would now rule over their wives and wives would look to their husbands for fulfillment. Biblical scholar Walter Kaiser states that the actual meaning of the Hebrew word *teshuqah* is "to turn to." When translated in this context as "desire," it speaks of the woman's tendency now to turn to Adam for her significance rather than to God. In transferring her loyalties from God to man, she will become vulnerable to the domination of men. This is an indication of sin, not a divine order established by God.

In contrast, here is how the popular *New Living Translation* (NLT) renders Genesis 3:16: "And you will desire *to control* (italics added) your husband, but he will rule over you."

What is astonishing here is that the translators of the NLT gave themselves permission to read into this passage their own theological presuppositions in interpreting "desire" as "desire to control." They took the liberty to interpret and paraphrase what they felt the text was saying rather than translating the text accurately from the original and leaving it to the reader to research and interpret the meaning of *teshuqah*. The ESV takes a similar liberty in their own interpretation of this passage: "Your desire shall be *contrary* (italics added) to your husband, but he shall rule over you."

Suggesting a woman wants to "control" her husband or is inclined to be "contrary" implies she is rebelling against a divinely established hierarchical relationship that predates the Fall. According to this thinking, sin has brought about a power struggle in which women will try to rebel against the God-ordained oversight of men, making it necessary for husbands to take charge and "rule over" their wives in order to achieve conformity to God's will and purpose. The implication is that any woman who wants to function with any kind of autonomy or equal status with men is being sinful.

Over the centuries, many Christians have come to believe that Genesis 3:16 gives men divine permission to rule and control their wives when in fact there is no divine mandate to justify such a belief. This tragic consequence of sin entering the world is descriptive, not prescriptive. It is to be understood as one of the consequences of the Fall similar to how God addresses Adam in the very next verses.

> Because you listened to your wife and ate fruit from the tree . . . cursed is the ground because of you; through painful toil you will eat food from it all the days of your life. It will produce

thorns and thistles for you . . . By the sweat of your brow you will eat your food until you return to the ground . . . (Genesis 3:17-19)

No complementarian preacher has ever suggested that God's original design for the man was a cursed ground and painful sweaty toil. God's words to Adam are understood by every biblical scholar to be a description of sin's sad consequences. To suggest otherwise for God's words to Eve just one verse earlier is to twist out of context any sound biblical exegesis of this passage.

Shifting Gears

Shifting to the New Testament, the translators of the NLT once again impose their theological position by deliberately paraphrasing certain passages to imply that the Scriptures don't allow for women to exercise spiritual authority or function as church leaders. While all Christians have the right to their own convictions, taking liberties in the translation to promote those convictions brings into question the reliability of their translation of Scripture.

For example, the New International Version (2011) accurately translates the qualifications for office of elder in 1 Timothy 3:1-2: "Whoever aspires to be an overseer desires a noble task. Now the overseer is to be above reproach."

Unfortunately, most English translations of 1 Timothy 3:1-6 give the impression that these qualifications for church leadership refer only to men. But in the original Greek text, no gender designation is used in this passage. "Whoever aspires to be an overseer" can refer to men or women.

The NLT completely ignores this fact in their translation: "If someone aspires to be an elder, he desires an honorable position. So an elder *must be a man* (italics added) whose life is above reproach."

This may sound straightforward, but the NLT translators have taken an enormous liberty in inserting the phrase "he . . . must be a man" into their version of verse 2. This phrase simply does not appear in any Greek manuscript.

In the same way, the ESV supports the concepts of male-only leadership by substituting masculine language in their translation rather than the gender-inclusive or gender-neutral found in the Greek text. In the next chapter I will limit my citations exclusively to the New Testament in giving you a small sampling of the many translational errors.

Chapter Seventeen

Turning a Blind Eye

According to Philippians 1:1, the church has only two official offices—that of elder and that of deacon. The apostle Paul was consistent in his letters with how he used the word *diakonos* or deacon. Unfortunately, the ESV translators were not. For instance, in 1 Timothy 3:8-13, the ESV translates *diakonos* as deacons or ministers when referring to men. But in Romans 16:1-2, where the apostle Paul refers to a woman named Phoebe as *diakonos*, the translators chose to translate the same Greek word as servant.

This disparity is also true in the New King James Version, which translates *diakonos* as minister when referring to men and as servant when referring to Phoebe. This despite clear documentation that Phoebe occupied the office of deacon in the early church.

Paul uses the word *diakonos* for people who were church leaders with a sacred commission. As such, *diakonoi* (plural) are described as being a *diakonos* of Christ such as Timothy (1 Timothy 4:6), of God (2 Corinthians 6:4), of the gospel (Ephesians 3:7), or of a specific local church. Not once does Paul use the word to refer to the general spiritual servanthood to which all believers are called. Rather, he typically used the term *diakonos* for Christian ministers.

These *diakonoi* included Paul himself (Romans 15:25, 1 Corinthians 3:5, Ephesians 3:7, Colossians 1:23, etc.), Timothy (1 Timothy 4:6), Epaphras (Colossians 1:7), Tychicus (Ephesians 6:21-22, Colossians 4:7-9), Apollos (1 Corinthians 3:5), and even Jesus Christ (Romans 15:8). And while not recognized by the translators of the ESV and some other versions, Paul refers to Phoebe, a woman, as *diakonos* of the church at Cenchrea, indicating she was indeed a leader or minister of that church.

"HE" IS A "SHE"

Paul further introduces us to another woman in Romans 16:7 named Junia, who is identified as an apostle. It is equally troubling to find the feminine name Junia changed in several translations to the masculine name Junius, an otherwise unknown male name. This unorthodox change was based solely on the assumption that a woman couldn't hold the office of apostle or elder (cf. 1 Peter 5:1; Peter was an apostle and elder). So the translators determined that the feminine name Junia must be a scribal error of some kind, thus the necessity of renaming her Junius. That solution temporarily addressed the seeming contradiction until a tidal wave of textual and historical evidence proved beyond a shadow of a doubt that this apostle was a woman whose name was indeed Junia.

Since Junia's identity as a woman has come to light, complementarians such as the translators of the ESV have endeavored to disavow her as an apostle through other means. First, despite a mountain of evidence affirming the name Junia as feminine, the ESV retains the alternate reading of Junius in a footnote for Romans 16:7. Another footnote for Romans 16:7 also suggests that the word apostle in this context just means a messenger, implying that both Andronicus and Junia were simply messengers.

There's more. In most English translations of Romans 16:7, Andronicus and Junia are referred to as "outstanding among the apostles" (Greek: *episēmos en tois apostolois*). But the ESV replaces the description of "outstanding among" (Greek: *episēmos en*) with "well-known to" the apostles. This implies that Andronicus and Junia were known by the apostles but not apostles themselves. One can only assume the reason the ESV has gone to this much trouble (two alternate footnotes and one misleading translation) is to obscure the fact that Junia was in fact a well-known female apostle.

The fourth-century church father John Chrysostom clearly acknowledged Junia as a female apostle when he wrote in his *Homily 31 on Romans*:

> And indeed to be apostles at all is a great thing. But to be even among these of note, just consider what a great tribute this is! But they were of note owing to their works, to their achievements. Oh! How great is the wisdom of this woman [Junia] that she should be counted worthy of the appellation of apostle!

Are "People" Only Men?

Many complementarians seem willing to go to great lengths to diminish the possibility that a woman could ever be a deacon, elder, or apostle though the New Testament never says a woman can't occupy these positions. Another such example in the ESV can be found in their translation of 2 Timothy 2:2.

> And what you have heard from me in the presence of many witnesses entrust to faithful men [*anthrōpoi*] who will be able to teach others also.

While the literal meaning of *anthrōpoi* is *people*, the ESV translates it here as *men*, presumably because of the reference to teaching. But in the very next chapter of the same epistle, the ESV translates the same term correctly as *people*.

> For people [*anthrōpoi*] will be lovers of self, lovers of money, proud, arrogant, abusive, disobedient to their parents, ungrateful, unholy. (2 Timothy 3:2)

Another example of this inconsistency in the ESV is seen in Ephesians 4:8, 11-12.

> Therefore it says, "When he ascended on high, he led a host of captives, and he gave gifts to men [*anthrōpoi*] . . . And he gave the apostles, the prophets, the evangelists, the shepherds and teachers, to equip the saints for the work of the ministry.

As just noted, the word *men* in this passage should read *people*, which includes women. Again, it appears that the translators are dismissing the possibility that women can be gifted as apostles, prophets, evangelists, shepherds, and teachers. In contrast, the NIV translates it accurately as *people* to include both men and women. A final example of such deliberate misinterpretation by the ESV can be found in Romans 12:1.

> I appeal to you therefore brothers, by the mercies of God, to present your bodies as a living sacrifice, holy and acceptable to God, which is your spiritual worship.

The ESV's own footnotes on Romans 12:1 admits that the Greek word here *adelphoi* should be translated as "brothers and sisters." Yet they have chosen not to do so. Paul is certainly referring to all members of the church in this verse. So why would a correct translation as "brothers and sisters" be omitted here?

Perhaps because Paul exhorts his audience in the following verses to exercise their spiritual gifts of prophecy, teaching, exhortation, and leadership? It appears that the ESV is once again downplaying the possibility that these gifts are given to both men and women. Greek scholar Mark L Strauss (the "Einstein" of New Testament translations) makes the following observation in his article "Why the English Standard Version Should Not Become the Standard English Version."

> One wonders why, if the ESV footnote acknowledges that *adelphoi* here means "brothers and sisters," it was not translated as such. The most likely answer is that the translators were concerned about their constituents who would have objected to this perceived condescension to a feminist agenda. All translation

is to some extent political, and in this case perhaps it was deemed necessary to sacrifice accuracy for expediency.

UNAPOLOGETICALLY COMPLEMENTARIAN

One of the most influential such constituents is the Council on Biblical Manhood and Womanhood (CBMW), a distinctively patriarchal-complementarian organization. They endorse the ESV by describing the translation as "unapologetically complementarian." This endorsement should immediately sound an alarm regarding the ESV's predisposition to read masculine interpretations into various passages.

Sadly, I (Eric) loved the ESV translation until I discovered this bias. Regarding doctrinal accuracy, it appeared exceptional. But now that I've seen for myself the deliberate gender discrimination used by its translators, my confidence in its reliability has been deeply shaken.

Let me further highlight my concern about the objectivity of ESV translators by drawing the reader's attention to the fact that ninety-five total theologians and scholars contributed to the *ESV Study Bible*. That represents a wide diversity of scholarship and denominational backgrounds. But guess how many of these biblical scholars were female? Twenty? Ten? Five? One?

How about zero! Not one woman was involved in the translation process of the ESV. They were all men. With literally hundreds of qualified female biblical scholars worldwide, one must wonder why not a single woman was chosen for this project. A background check into the list of contributors to the *ESV Study Bible* reveals that the majority were hierarchical complementarians. And it isn't just the ninety-five contributors to the *ESV Study Bible* that were all male. All members of the ESV oversight committee as well as the review scholars were male. Political indeed! For me these are blatant examples of gender injustice taking place at the highest levels of the Church.

I can no longer trust the ESV when it comes to how they translate verses related to woman in general and to women in church leadership specifically. I believe that many women growing up today in both westernized cultures and developing nations are learning falsehoods about what the Bible teaches regarding the roles of men and women. Many conclude that Christianity, and therefore God, demeans women.

As a result, women reject Christianity, not because they don't find the message of the gospel attractive, but because they can't accept a religion that treats women as second-class persons. These unbiblical biases taught from pulpits and even mistranslated in the Bible have led to the belief that role limitations imposed on girls and women is divinely sanctioned. This is *not* without consequences.

In Christian homes, such teachings erode the healthy boundaries of wives and daughters and engender a sense of passivity and feeling of powerlessness. Wives tolerate treatment from their husbands that is damaging to their mutual relationship as well as relationships with their children. They learn to suppress their instinct to be advocates for themselves or for their children because they believe it's unbiblical to confront or disagree with their husbands.

THE GREATER EVIDENCE

In his 1186-page tome *Christian Theology* that I (Eric) was required to read in seminary, remarkable Christian thinker and theologian Millard Erickson addresses the question of whether women can hold leadership positions in the church. After examining carefully arguments on both sides of this issue, he concluded with an assessment that reflects my own thinking on this controversial subject.

> In my judgment, the evidence is not clear-cut in support of either position alone. On balance, however, ***the greater evidence*** (italics added) appears to support the position of full access to [all] these ministries for women. (pg. 1007, Christian Theology, Third Edition)

For thirty-one years as a lead teaching pastor, I referred to myself as "a pragmatic fanatic." In using that term, I was attempting to describe myself as someone who looked for practical ways to empower the church to achieve the greatest good. In retrospect, I now see that I was neither pragmatic nor fanatic when it came to the issue of empowering women to serve and lead within the local church. On this very critical issue, I failed to achieve the greatest good.

Today when the church desperately needs qualified pastors, teachers, evangelists, administrators, elders, and deacons, many church leaders are choosing to simply avoid the issue of women in leadership. In doing so, we are acting less than courageously. In failing to embrace the leadership of women, we have denied the church a huge percentage of its workforce, robbing the church of the benefits of their spiritual gifts and talents simply because they are female.

I believe in many ways the church has limped along for centuries with only half of the image of God being presented to the world. Pastor Paul Yonggi Cho, pastor emeritus of Yoido Full Gospel Church in Seoul, South Korea, the largest church in the world (over 800,000) once addressed this point eloquently.

> They ask me, "What's the key to your church?" I tell them again, "Release your women." But they just don't hear me.

Paul's Ministry Partners

There are women today who resent the apostle Paul and believe his writings are intrinsically oppressive toward women. But the opposite is actually true. Contrary to the mistaken assumption that Paul prohibited women leaders in the church, he followed in Jesus's footsteps and continued the emancipation of women, giving them the same authority as men to carry out the ministry. The inaccurate perception that Paul discriminated against women is the result of a handful of verses being taken out of context and used incorrectly.

At least eighteen women are mentioned in the Pauline epistles. Sixteen are identified by name. Most of these women are mentioned independently of a man, though some are listed along with a male relative. Here is a list in alphabetical order of the eighteen women mentioned in Paul's letters. Apphia (Philemon 1:2), Chloe (1 Corinthians 1:11), Claudia (2 Timothy 4:21), Eunice (2 Timothy 1:5), Euodia (Philippians 4:2-3), Julia (Romans 16:15), Junia (Romans 16:7, NIV), Lois (2 Timothy 1:5), Mary (Romans 16:6), Nereus's sister (Romans 16:15), Nympha (Colossians 4:15), Persis (Romans 16:12), Phoebe (Romans 16:1-2, NIV), Priscilla (Romans 16:3-5, 1 Corinthians 16:19, 2 Timothy 4:19, cf. Acts 18:1-3, 18-19, 26), Rufus's mother (Romans 16:13), Syntyche (Philippians 4:2-3), Tryphena (Romans 16:12), Tryphosa (Romans 16:12). Lydia is also mentioned in Acts 16:13-15, 40.

Throughout his writings, Paul uses the same terms of ministry—coworker, deacon/minister (*diakonos*), apostle—for both male and female colleagues. The significance of this can hardly be overemphasized. In Romans 16 alone, we find Paul greeting twenty-nine individuals who had participated with him in the ministry of the gospel. Ten of these are women.

What is especially interesting is that seven of these ten women are given specific designations identifying their ministry (apostle, deacon, or partner in ministry.) By comparison, only three of the men in this passage are given a designation, and two of these are identified as ministering alongside their wives. These are numbers worth remembering. Considering the culture of the time that gave women fewer freedoms than men, seven out of twenty-nine is a considerable number of women in ministry.

What's perhaps more significant here is that more women in Romans 16 are described by or commended for their ministries than men—seven women compared with three men. What this implies as to the balance between male and female leadership, we can't really extrapolate from the information given. But what is certain is that women were active in significant ministries in the church at Rome and that the apostle Paul had no problem with these women being ministers. Rather, he affirmed them and their ministries, acknowledging his acceptance of women in leadership.

Chapter Eighteen

The Silent Treatment

Very few people familiar with the Bible are unaware of the Pauline directive that women are to be silent in the church. 1 Corinthians 14:34-35 is one of the most notable passages used by opponents of a woman's right to speak and teach in church. There we find the thrice repeated admonition: "Let your women keep silence in the churches" (KJV). Or as the New Living Translation renders it: "Women should be silent during the church meetings."

Whether you read these verses in the King James Version or a modern translation, a passing glance appears to represent a clear injunction against a woman's verbal involvement in church services. Armed with superficial understanding of such passages, the male leadership of many churches believes this sanction against women has been signed, sealed, and delivered by God himself. It is impossible to fully calculate the devastating impact these misunderstood words have had on the leadership development of women called to serve within the Christian community.

The irony is that it is virtually unfeasible this was Paul's intended meaning when first penned. As with all biblical interpretation, "a text without a context is a pretext." In other words, without a knowledge of the historical and cultural context of a passage of Scripture, it can be easily misinterpreted. Two problems at least with the traditional "women must be silent" interpretation immediately jump out. Understanding them at even an elementary level will render a much different perception of their true meaning.

UNFAIRLY SINGLED OUT

First, the "must be silent" interpretation directly contradicts Paul's statements in this same chapter. In 1 Corinthians 14:5, 24, 26, 31, we are told that "all" or "everyone" or "each one" (clearly including women believers) may sing, speak, share spiritual insights, teach, and prophesy. We also read in 1 Corinthians 11:5 that women could pray and prophesy publicly in the church. Why would Paul affirm and allow women to pray and prophesy in 1 Corinthians 11, then three chapters later contradict himself by prohibiting women from even speaking in church?

Clearly then, this passage is not about keeping women from speaking and teaching in the church. A closer look at what was taking place in the Corinthian church gives clarity about what Paul was actually saying. Without question, the primary focus of Paul's writing here was the disorderly way congregational meetings were being conducted in Corinth. It appears that various members felt their newfound liberty in Christ permitted free expression however and whenever they desired. Prophecy, speaking in tongues, and sharing various revelations spontaneously during the service had all led to a lack of order and edification. Thus the need for apostolic guidelines to quell the chaos.

While women are often unfairly singled out as the main contributors to this confusion, Paul admonished in this chapter several individuals and groups who were responsible for the disorder and confusion taking place. In verses 27–28a, he told those speaking in tongues that if there was no one to interpret these utterances, then those speaking them should "keep silent in church." Paul then moves on to address prophets in the church.

> Let two or three prophets speak, and let the others weigh what is said. If a revelation is made to another sitting there, let the first be silent for you can all prophesy one by one. The spirits of prophets are subject to the control of prophets. For God is not a God of disorder but of peace—as in all the congregations of the Lord's people. (1 Corinthians 14: 29–33)

Note that Paul's admonishment to the prophets is specifically linked to disorderly conduct in the services and that once again he gives the injunction to "be silent." Only after these two prior groups have been admonished does he address the women as a group.

> Women should remain silent in the churches. They are not allowed to speak, but must be in submission, as the law says. If they want to inquire about something, they should ask their own husbands at home; for it is disgraceful for a woman to speak in the church. (1 Corinthians 14: 34-35)

Stopping the Confusion

All three of these prohibitions were aimed at solving the same problem—establishing order and proper etiquette for public worship services. Women, not unlike other members of the congregation manifesting gifts, were to refrain from publicly asking questions that disrupted the service. This is particularly significant because the women of Paul's time, like many places in the developing world today, were often denied the formal education men were privileged to receive. Most lower-class women were illiterate and had little knowledge of the Old Testament scriptures on which early church teaching was based. Men and women also sat separately in the gathering place, so asking their husbands a question during the service would also be disruptive.

A Present-Day Illustration

An experience a missionary friend shared with me might offer additional clarification for this passage. She and her husband were visiting a new village church plant in central India with a group of Indian Christian leaders that included several women, one a dentist, the other a doctor working for India's health service, all well-educated and experienced Bible teachers.

In contrast, the two hundred plus believers squeezed into this small concrete sanctuary were of an extremely impoverished rural tribal group. The women sat packed like sardines on shawls and rugs on one side of the sanctuary while the men sat on the other. A few of the men had Bibles open on their crossed legs, but none of the women could read and many only spoke their tribal language, not the regional language into which the visiting missionary's sermon was being translated—and which the men had learned in school and through interaction with the wider society. While the men and those women who understood were listening attentively to the sermon, other women, uncomprehending and bored, began whispering to each other, asking what the preacher was saying, playing with their infants, digging out food to feed toddlers, and in general making enough noise that it was hard to listen to the speaker.

That was when my missionary friend noticed two of the church deacons walking through the packed crowd on the sanctuary floor with a rod in their hands. Leaning over the seated women, they would tap chattering offenders on the shoulder with their rod and hiss sharply, "Be silent! Be respectful! Let our brother speak God's Word! If you don't understand, ask your husband when you get home!"

When my missionary friend shared this story with us, I thought of how this was very likely a similar scene to what Paul had in mind when penning his admonition to these women in Corinth. As in this Indian village church, the Corinthian women would also have been largely illiterate, uneducated in Scripture, and unable to follow teaching that their better educated husbands—and even higher-class women in the same congregation—could. Which in no way prevented gifted women like Priscilla, Lydia, and so many others from studying and teaching the Scriptures. Or women believers in general from sharing a word from God in an orderly, respectful fashion that didn't disrupt services—exactly as Paul had already admonished two other segments of the congregation.

The overall context makes it clear that 1 Corinthians 14:34-35 is not a prohibition against women speaking or teaching in the church but applies specifically to the issue of members whose behavior was disrupting the service. Unfortunately, the "silent treatment" still speaks loud and clear in the minds of many Christians, joining the chorus of other misinterpreted verses that suggest male privilege and even superiority.

A Church-Specific Prohibition

While some complementarians may concede to the above interpretation of 1 Corinthians 14, most believe there is a "mother" of all verses that presents irrefutable proof a woman may not preach or teach in the church. Here is that passage as translated in the ESV.

> A woman should learn in quietness and full submission. I do not permit a woman to teach or to assume authority over a man; she must be quiet. (1 Timothy 2:11-12)

At a surface level, this passage appears an absolute, timeless principle that would prohibit women from ever teaching or having authority within the church. But this one passage doesn't tell the entire story, and a proper understanding of its context makes evident that it is neither a universal prohibition nor should be used to forbid women from serving as pastors, elders, and teachers within the contemporary Christian community. In fact, Paul's statement here in 1 Timothy 2:12 must be understood as a circumstantial and local church-specific prohibition. Here are three compelling reasons why this is true.

First, those claiming this passage supports patriarchy do so while ignoring centuries of biblical revelation. Down through redemptive history, God frequently called upon women to rise above oppressive patriarchic cultures to take a position of influence and leadership in advancing his kingdom. We've already looked at a number of these women like Miriam, Deborah, Ruth, Esther, the prophet Hulda, and others. Another we haven't even discussed is the prophet Anna who encountered Joseph and Mary when they took the infant Jesus to the temple for his consecration rites as a first-born son (Luke 2:36-38). So how is it possible that God himself would raise up numerous women to judge, prophecy, teach, direct, advise, and lead men in countless capacities, only to turn around and in one verse contradict his own directives?

God is the one who chose these women, and whatever God chooses to do cannot be considered intrinsically wrong. So that Paul is prohibiting women in this particular letter to Timothy from holding positions of leadership or authority indicates that circumstantial factors are in play and not a universally binding principle. In teaching hermeneutics (the methodology of interpreting Scripture), I constantly warned about the hazard of using a single or obscure passage to interpret other passages that are clear and consistent. This foundational principle in biblical interpretation can be summarized from the words of the Westminster Confession of Faith (1:7, 9).

> All things in Scripture are not alike plain in themselves, nor alike clear unto all. When there is a question about the true and full sense of any Scripture . . . it must be searched and known by other places that speak more clearly.

What the Reformers were saying here is that we must always begin with the explicit teaching of Scripture, then move to the implicit. Interpreting the clear with the unclear is the basis for the false teachings of many heretics and cults. While some speak as though 1 Timothy 2:9-13 is indeed a clear and unambiguous passage, the notorious difficulties of the text have generated a multitude of technical articles and thousands of pages discussing its difficulties.

IDEOLOGICAL HUMILITY

Steve Clifford, pastor of Westgate Church in San Jose, California, makes the following observation.

> After four years of studying this whole issue, I'm still not sure what 1 Timothy 2:12 means. And I will tell you something else. I don't trust anybody who is sure. There are just too many variables to know exactly what Paul meant. Complementarians, do I know for sure what's going on? I do not know for sure, but I don't think that you can know for sure [either].

The ideological humility shown here by Pastor Clifford is laudable. The unique composition of this passage and its ambiguities invalidates the use of this verse as the definitive key to unlocking all other passages regarding women's roles in the church. Especially when contrasted with the many, many passages of Scripture that highlight and extol the influential roles of women as normative for the church over all time.

One complementarian writer opposed that conclusion, saying:

> How many times does God's Word have to say something for it to be true? Once is enough. Therefore, the argument that the command in 1 Timothy 2:12 does not apply universally to the church because such a teaching occurs only once is false.

We agree that God needs to say something only once for it to be true. But he would not do so if that utterance was in contradiction of what has already been clearly affirmed in Scripture. That said, this writer does make one good point: "such a teaching occurs only once."

Therein lies its weakness. To exalt the uncertain meaning of this passage against example after example that demonstrate the opposite must be considered ill-advised. We acknowledge that God can make himself exceedingly clear on any given subject with only one statement or commandment. But this passage isn't one of them. Clearly it is unwise for interpreters to be dogmatic in their interpretation of 1 Timothy 2:12.

Chapter Nineteen

A Red Flag

Which brings us to our second compelling reason why 1 Timothy 2:12 doesn't exclude qualified women from church leadership. The verse uses an extremely unique and rare word for "exercise authority." It is the word *authentein*.

Saying this word is rare is an understatement. Theologians refer to it as a *hapax legomenon*, which means that the word only appears one time in the entire biblical record. In fact, Paul goes outside the Bible to borrow the word from the vernacular of the contemporary culture. This in turn makes it impossible to determine its exact meaning by comparing it with other biblical passages.

This alone should immediately present the reader with a red flag. As mentioned above, one must be extremely cautious about creating a normative biblical absolute from any single verse. This is especially true when the verse uses such a unique word.

Additionally, this verse has been poorly translated in such Bible versions as the English Standard Version and the New American Standard Bible, where *authentein* is rendered in a neutral sense such as "have authority" or "exercise authority." Even a cursory understanding of the word *authentein* in its historical context makes these translations highly unlikely and with significant implications as to the bias behind the choice of wording. John Jeffery Davis, Ph.D. in his article "First Timothy 2:12, the Ordination of Women, and Paul's Use of Creation Narratives" sums up the issue.

> Prior to and contemporary with the first century, *authentein* often had negative overtones such as "domineer" or even "murder" or "perpetrate a crime." Only during the later patristic period did the meaning "to exercise authority" come to predominate... Paul could easily have chosen to use the ordinary Greek word for leadership and authority, *proistemi*. This word occurs eight times in the New Testament and is used six times by Paul in reference to church leaders (1 Timothy 3:4-5, 12; 5:17; 1 Thessalonians 5:12, Romans 12:8). *Proistemi* means "to manage, conduct, rule, direct, be concerned about." But instead of the normal word for authority, Paul uses the unique and ambiguous word *authentein* (indicating excessive force) to describe this restriction placed upon women in the church at Ephesus.

Cynthia Long Westfall adds clarity to the meaning of *authentein* in her 2016 book *Paul and Gender: Reclaiming the Apostle's Vision for Men and Women in Christ*.

> In the Greek corpus, the verb *authenteō* refers to a range of actions that are not restricted to murder or violence. However, the people who are targets of these actions are harmed, forced against their will (compelled), or at least their self-interest is being

overridden because the actions involve an imposition of the subject's will ranging from dishonor to lethal force.

SHE'S JUST TOO PUSHY!

The use of the word *authentein* for authority points to the fact that it meant to aggressively seize power or dominate another and had very negative connotations in the first century. *Authentein* is translated as "domineer" in the Latin Vulgate and New English Bible and as "usurp authority" in the Geneva and King James Bibles. The etymology of the word *authentein* verifies its aggressive nature, *autos* meaning "self" while *entea* translates as "arm" or "armor." It means "to unilaterally take up arms, to self-arm for battle, i.e. acting as an autocrat – literally self-appointed and acting without submission."

So Paul is setting forth here a directive to a woman or group of women who were using illegitimate authority to force their false teachings upon the believers in Ephesus. They were teaching in a domineering way. Timothy is commanded to stop this type of aggressive and coercive effort and to direct these women to "learn in quietness" before they could be qualified to teach anyone else.

The highly unusual word Paul uses here in 1 Timothy 2:12 would be consistent with an unusual set of circumstances to which the text is addressing. It is likely that Paul was objecting to something other than the legitimate use of authority. For that reason, many scholars believe that there was an uncommon and specific abuse of authority taking place in Ephesus. In both First and Second Timothy, there are strong indications of women being deceived and led away by false teachers (1 Timothy 1:3-7; 4:1-7; 6:3-5, 20-21, 2 Timothy 2:14-18, 23-26; 3:1-9). In some cases, the women were themselves becoming false teachers. As such, those women were not to be allowed to "teach or usurp authority." They were clearly not suitable to have authority over anyone in the church.

The passage teaches silence for women who have not yet been taught or who have been taught incorrectly. Once properly taught and trained, these women like other mature believers would no longer be "usurping authority" when given the opportunity to teach. Paul's decision to use the word *authentein* was deliberate and never meant to limit women who are called by God and appointed by the church to serve in positions of teaching and leadership.

It is also important to note that the word typically translated "be silent" (*siōpaō/sigaō*, meaning silence/silent) is not used in 1 Timothy 2:11-12. The word used is *hesuchia*, which refers more to a disposition of calmness, tranquility, or being settled rather than total silence. Paul wasn't saying these women should be completely silent but that they needed to settle down and learn in a submissive manner, the proper conduct of any good student. Nevertheless, several English versions translate the word in this particular passage as "silence/silent" (KJV, HCSB, NIV 1984, RSV, NRSV for example).

PERMISSION GRANTED

We've given two reasons for understanding that 1 Timothy 2:12-13 doesn't disqualify women from exercising authority over men as teachers. First, this one verse is an inadequate basis to forbid women from teaching when many other verses affirm that qualified women may exercise leadership in the church. Secondly, the word for authority (*authentein*), unique to all other uses of that word in Scripture, denotes the use of force and aggression. The context is clear that Paul is addressing a problem of certain unqualified women who were imposing false teaching in a domineering manner.

So let's examine our third compelling reason why 1 Timothy 2:12-13 doesn't exclude qualified women from church leadership. Some complementarians suggest that the chronological order of creation establishes Adam's superiority over Eve. They assert that man's hierarchical standing justifies why women shouldn't be teaching men. In addition, the deception of Eve is cited as evidence of women's moral and emotional weakness, even inferiority to men, the conclusion being that women are not suitable or acceptable as teachers in the body of Christ. They use the following verse to support this view.

> For Adam was formed first, then Eve; and Adam was not deceived, but the woman was deceived and became a transgressor. (1 Timothy 2:13)

As mentioned earlier, one immediate problem with this interpretation is that nothing in the first two chapters of Genesis implies Adam's ascendancy and preeminence over Eve or her moral and intellectual inferiority to Adam. To the contrary, this idea of a binding hierarchical relationship between men and women is disproven by the pre-Fall narrative itself. There is not the slightest hint, not a whisper, regarding a formal arrangement where men are ranked above women in the creation account or seen as morally superior to them. The creation order establishes equality and oneness, not hierarchy and superiority (Genesis 2:24).

SHAKY GROUND

So a claim that Paul's reference to the creation/Fall narrative supports male primacy stands on shaky ground. Such interpretation doesn't give adequate thought to numerous other references Paul makes to the creation texts, each one revealing a different perspective in the context-specific situations Paul addresses throughout his letters. Linking this creation model reference to a prohibition of all women from teaching is certainly questionable.

In reflecting on Paul's reference to the creation/Fall narratives, we see at least six diverse uses of them in his letters (Romans 5:12-21; 14:14, 20-21, 1 Corinthians 11:8, 2 Corinthians 11:3, 1 Timothy 2:13; 4:1-5.) In each, Paul applies various aspects of the creation/Fall narrative to the unique theological and situational challenges faced by each congregation. For example, while in 1 Timothy 2:13 Eve is said to have been deceived, Romans 5:12-21 cites Adam, not Eve, as the one whose sin brought death and destruction upon the entire world (Genesis 3:17-19). In fact, of the six times Paul uses this creation/Fall narrative to address an issue, Eve is only mentioned in two of them.

Another situational application of the creation narrative can be seen in Romans 14, which deals with food offered to idols. Based on Genesis 1:29-30, Paul states that "nothing is unclean in itself" (Romans 14:14) and that "all food is clean" (Romans 14:20). Nevertheless, he urges Gentile believers in Rome to refrain from eating meat if it "causes your brother to stumble" (Romans 14:21). In other words, though the creation narrative makes clear that God created all foods to be "good," Paul makes a prohibitive application because of a specific problem in the Roman church, urging Gentile believers to forego their freedom and "not destroy the work of God for the sake of food" (Romans 14: 20).

In contrast, we find a very different application of the same creation narrative in Paul's letter to Timothy directed to the church in Ephesus (1 Timothy 4:1-5). Instead of urging believers not to eat certain foods for fear of causing a brother to stumble, Paul encourages them not to refrain from eating anything. Why this unusual change of emphasis? In Ephesus Paul was responding to false teachers who were imposing extra-biblical dietary restrictions that had absolutely nothing to do with the gospel. So he urges the believers to enjoy their freedom in Christ and to eat all types of food, stating that "everything created by God is good and nothing is to be rejected if it is received with thanksgiving" (1 Timothy 4:4). It should be noted that this is the same church and same letter Paul writes to Timothy where he warns Timothy of women who were clearly causing trouble as false teachers.

In another example, Paul warns the church in Corinth of a very real danger that the entire congregation might be deceived by false teachers.

> I am afraid that just as Eve was deceived by the serpent's cunning, your minds may somehow be led astray from your sincere and pure devotion to Christ. (2 Corinthians 11:3)

In this reference, Paul draws a parallel between Eve's deception and the entire Corinthian congregation. There is nothing gender specific about his application or an implication that women are more susceptible to deception. Rather, Eve is used here as a warning to both men and women within the Corinthian church. This contrasts with 1 Timothy 2:13 where Paul uses Eve as a warning to specific women who were creating problems in the church of Ephesus.

ONE SIZE FITS ALL?

This variation once again demonstrates how Paul is using the creation/Fall narrative to speak to specific problems in various congregations rather than to establish an absolute and binding principle. Dr. John Jefferson Davis again describes in his article the contrast between 2 Corinthians 11:3 and 1 Timothy 2:13.

> This comparison of 2 Corinthians 11:3 and 1 Timothy 2:13 shows that Paul does not have a "one size fits all" hermeneutic when reading and applying the Genesis narratives of creation and fall: Eve can be seen as a figure of *women* in Ephesus or as a figure for *an entire church* in Corinth—because the local circumstances differ though false teaching is a danger in both settings. Applications are drawn from Genesis in a church-specific and contextually sensitive way.

To understand Paul's thinking here, it is essential to understand the context of his first letter to Timothy. From the beginning chapter, he poses false teaching as the reason Timothy was left in Ephesus (1 Timothy 1:3-7). This concern continues throughout both First and Second Timothy, indicating that women were being victimized by these false teachers. The most explicit reference is found in 2 Timothy 3:6-7 which speaks of "those who creep into households and capture weak women burdened with sins and led astray by various passions, who are always learning and never able to arrive at a knowledge of the truth" (see also 1 Timothy 1:19-20; 4:1-3, 7; 5:6-16; 6:3-5, 20-21, 2 Timothy 2:14-18, 23-26; 3:1-9, 13; 4:3-4, 14-15).

This problem was so pronounced that Paul cites the example of younger widows who had already "turned away to follow Satan" (1 Timothy 5:15). This gives us certainty that the prohibition concerning women was to correct a very specific alarming problem in Ephesus. It is also worth noting that other than the misinterpreted "women be silent" verse in 1 Corinthians 14:34-35, no other prohibitions about women teaching can be found anywhere in the New Testament.

Considering the witness of other scriptures and the unique grammar and situational context, 1 Timothy 2:12-13 cannot be used to prohibit woman from teaching. While it may be argued that Paul's appeal to the basic order of creation supersedes the situational or cultural context, this basis for male superiority over women is ill-informed. In fact, the creation of men and women in the image of God argue for the exact opposite interpretation.

Chapter Twenty

For Better or For Worse?

History shows that human beings have a profound tendency to dominant and control others. James explains our power struggles this way.

> Where do you think all these appalling wars and quarrels come from? Do you think they just happen? Think again. They come about because you want your own way, and fight for it deep inside yourselves. (James 4:1, *The Message*)

This desire to impose our will on others leads to hurt feelings, isolation, and even abuse. Having to win every argument, be in the right, or prove your perspective is superior to your partner's is the stuff of broken relationships. Especially when this inclination shows up in the marriage relationship. It's no wonder G.K. Chesterton said, "Marriage is an adventure—like going to war."

Speaking of "going to war", we know from personal experience how the consequences of the Fall and growing up in very dysfunctional families can raise its ugly head in a multitude of ways in marriage. Before launching into a theological discussion on the most comprehensive and provocative biblical passage on marriage, we want to share how Christian patriarchy affected our indisputably challenging relationship. Early in our marriage, Eric and I (Carol) could have been a poster couple for what a dysfunctional and seemingly incompatible relationship looked like.

In many weddings, a daunting question is asked of the bride and groom. In ours it went something like this: "Eric, do you take Carol for better or for worse?" Once Eric responded with the expected "I do," the same question was asked of me (Carol). A standing joke between us has been that our marriage exceeded our expectations of being even worse than we took each other for. I'm thinking other couples can relate to that feeling.

An Ocean of Troubled Waters

Going into marriage, we assumed that as sincere Christians in full-time ministry we could negotiate the inevitable ups and downs of our relationship. We assumed marriage would be smooth sailing if we just followed God's prescribed plan. The problem was that the plan we tried to follow wasn't necessarily God's after all. Eric and I ended up with an ocean of troubled waters to navigate, in part to inaccurate theology and the imposed paradigm of hierarchy. What started out as a commitment to love, cherish, honor, and respect became a battle ground as our relationship became defined by expectations neither of us could live up to.

Christian stereotypes did our relationship no favors. When it came to decision making, I was more pragmatic and decisive while

Eric was more idealistic and cautious. Yet according to Christian patriarchy he was supposed to be the one leading the way. He would often avoid engaging in a discussion of differing perspectives, leaving me feeling frustrated. While I wanted him to understand my point of view, he often saw it as undermining his leadership. It wasn't long before much of the fun and spontaneity in our relationship became a distant, faint memory as we tried to side-step issues and just get along.

What happened to the friendship? Somewhere along the way it got lost in our attempts to follow the prescribed model of Christian patriarchy. Although I was better at managing finances, for Eric to be "head of the house" meant him taking charge in that area. While I balanced the books, when it came to having equal input on financial expenditures, suddenly Eric's role as the leader in our marriage would take precedent. He'd been taught that was the "manly" thing to do if he was going to "wear the pants" in our relationship.

Till Death Do Us Part

In many ways we couldn't have planned a more incongruent complementarian marriage. It became very apparent we'd never be happy trying to conform to the typical hierarchical model. We could either abandon the model and begin accepting and respecting each other's strengths and weaknesses irrespective of gender, or we could continue failing painfully to meet its expectations. Since divorce was never an option, we decided to work on building a different model for our relationship. A model that would honor our commitment to the biblical priority of love and mutual respect.

Simultaneously, Eric and I chose to invest in our happiness by seeking outside help. The professional counselors we met with coached us in how to resolve conflicts through collaboration while individually working on our own emotional unhealthiness and brokenness. The healthy approach to conflict resolution was not found by me submitting and him being in charge. It was into this new dimension of healthy emotional spirituality that Eric and I began our journey of healing. Our commitment "to death do us part" began to pay off as we jettisoned some of the ill-prescribed role expectations. Demonstrating mutual love and respect became the priority in our lifelong commitment to each other.

We will soon be approaching fifty years of marriage and have considered how we might renew our vows. I read about one couple who demonstrated their commitment to a biblical egalitarian marriage by washing each other's feet at their wedding. This type of giving and receiving, leading and submitting is something Jesus modeled when he washed his disciples' feet but also had his own feet washed by a beloved disciple, who happened to be a woman (Luke 7:44). The couple also modeled their mutual submission by challenging each other in their exchange of vows to honor the Lordship of Jesus in their life and marriage. Not sure that Eric would go for a foot washing, but knowing how much he likes to preach, he might agree to that one.

Looking back, it is clear to us what appeared to be irreconcilable differences could have been worked through with greater grace had we known then what we know now. Without ill-fitting roles touted as specific assignments from God, we would have been much happier having a relationship more closely aligned with God's original plan. Rather than grieving the "what could have been," we now look forward to our future together where love can flourish rather than being crushed under the weight of role expectations.

There was a time that I couldn't have even imagined Eric and I speaking together about marriage because of our own pain and unhealthiness. It is no less than a miracle that we've since conducted numerous marriage seminars together. We are a living testimony to how any sincere couple can be rescued from the indoctrination of harmful patriarchal teaching. We are now much more at ease with each other. There is much more spontaneity and fun in our relationship.

In lots of ways, we have naturally adapted to an egalitarian relationship where there is mutual love and respect. Eric no longer needs to remind me he is the leader. I no longer need to remind him how he is failing as a leader (ha-ha!). In fact, we now admire one another's leadership styles with differing gifts and abilities that function best in different aspects of our partnership. Now we can say that our marriage is for the better and not for the worse.

How Holy is Matrimony?

As a pastor, I (Eric) did my fair share of counseling couples through marital conflicts, having had plenty of personal experience in our own marriage. So how common is our natural tendency to have power struggles in marriage? It's as common as sunshine on a cloudless day. It's universal. It's omnipresent.

As destructive as this wayward inclination is, it is intensified exponentially in marriage when supported by a theology that encourages imperfect, sinful husbands to assume power over their wives. Many fine complementarian teachers have made gallant efforts to minimize the potential collateral damage and harmful consequences associated with their hierarchical viewpoint. Unfortunately, the end results are still a less than optimum environment for a man and woman to thrive in a marriage relationship.

On one occasion, a man marched his wife into my office and asked me to tell her to submit to him. I wanted to say, "You've got to be kidding!" Instead, I dove under my desk until the screaming subsided and she stopped throwing things (not literally!). This man's perilous demand was based on a passage often used to establish the husband's authority over his wife.

> Wives, submit to your own husbands, as to the Lord. For the husband is the head of the wife even as Christ is the head of the church, his body, and is himself its Savior. Now as the church submits to Christ, so also wives should submit in everything to their husbands.
>
> Husbands, love your wives, as Christ loved the church and gave himself up for her, that he might sanctify her, having cleansed her by the washing of water with the word, so that he might present the church to himself in splendor, without spot or wrinkle or any such thing, that she might be holy and without

blemish. In the same way husbands should love their wives as their own bodies. He who loves his wife loves himself. For no one ever hated his own flesh, but nourishes and cherishes it, just as Christ does the church, because we are members of his body. "

Therefore, a man shall leave his father and mother and hold fast to his wife, and the two shall become one flesh." This mystery is profound, and I am saying that it refers to Christ and the Church. However, let each one of you love his wife as himself, and let the wife see that she respects her husband. (Ephesians 5:22-33)

Complementarians hold the position that failure in marriage results when the roles of husbands and wives are not understood or played out biblically based on the above passage. They might suggest a wife's resistance or rebellion makes it impossible for her husband to be the leader he is supposed to be. Or that the husband is either unwilling to assume his role or being too harsh in dominating his wife. In our experience, much of the trouble in Christian marriages has been the direct result of misunderstanding this passage.

The Missing Key

One important key to understanding the Ephesians 5 passage is typically omitted. The verse just before this passage reads, "Submit to one another out of reverence for Christ" (v. 21). Everything that follows should be filtered through this command. Paul's clear intention was to introduce this dynamic discussion by first focusing on the mutual submission to which we are all called.

To compound this error, Bible publishers have often placed their own titles separating verses 21 and 22. In the NASB, the heading reads, "Marriage Like Christ and the Church". In the ESV, the title "Wives and Husbands" has been inserted. The impression given is that verse 22 is introducing a brand-new thought that is completely separate from verse 21. The New Living Translation shows greater scholarship in incorporating verses 21-33 under the heading "Spirit-Guided Relationships: Wives and Husbands." In the NLT, verses 21-25 reads:

> And further, submit to one another out of reverence for Christ. For wives, this means submit to your husbands as to the Lord . . . For husbands, this means love your wives, just as Christ loved the church. He gave up his life for her.

When we look at how these two verses (v. 21 and v. 22) relate in the original Greek it becomes infinitely clear that Paul's focus is on *mutual submission in marriage*. Verse 22 isn't even a complete sentence but an inseparable continuation of verse 21. In the original Greek, the word submit doesn't even appear in verse 22, which reads as a continuation of verse 21: "wives to your husband as to the Lord." Translators have simply borrowed the word "submit" from verse 21 where both the man and woman are exhorted to be in submission to one another. Which means that the marital instructions in verses 22-33 flow out of the exhortation of mutual submission in verse 21. The importance of this in understanding how a Christian marriage should work cannot be overemphasized.

The Lens of Mutual Submission

Looking at everything Paul says regarding wives and husbands through the lens of mutual submission changes everything. Mutual submission means it's impossible for one partner to be more powerful or privileged in the relationship. The good news of the gospel includes the restoration of creation conditions to male and female relationships. Since the concept of submission by the woman to the man as her superior wasn't part of the original creation account, it isn't meant to be a part of the New Creation either. Mutual submission to one another is the ideal model for Kingdom relationships.

That said, husbands and wives are individually addressed in Ephesians 5 about specific attitudes and behaviors. Wives are to respect their husbands. Husbands are to love their wives sacrificially. This can't possibly mean wives are exempt from being loving and nurturing towards their husbands or husbands exempt from being supportive and respectful towards their wives. In fact, it is worth noting that Ephesians 5 opens with a universal call for all believers to love sacrificially as Christ loves.

> Follow God's example, therefore, as dearly loved children and walk in the way of love, just as Christ loved us and gave himself up for us as a fragrant offering and sacrifice to God. (Ephesians 5:1-2).

The Bible records over fifty "one another" verses, each an exhortation on how to relate to each other out of Christ-like love. Here are just a few examples.

- John 13:14: Wash *one another*'s feet.

- Romans 12:10: Honor *one another* above yourselves.

- Romans 15:14: Instruct *one another*.

- 1 Corinthians 12:25: Have equal concern for *one another*.

- Galatians 5:13: Serve *one another*.

- Philippians 2:3: In humility consider *others* better than yourselves.

- Colossians 3:16: Admonish *one another*.

These expressions should not be disregarded when you enter holy matrimony. They are to be modeled in the Christian marriage even more adamantly.

Chapter Twenty-One

Two Words Say It All

In this next section, we are going to unpack two key words that unlock the true essence of Ephesians 5: "submit" and "head." After establishing mutual submission, Paul basically says, "Ladies first." Beginning in verse 22, Paul invites wives to submit to their husbands, then goes on to describe what that submission looks like in marriage. Read correctly, the verse is saying, "Wives submit yourselves to your own husbands as you do to the Lord."

The emphasis here is on the wife yielding, not the husband demanding. No one, male or female, is to rule over anyone else in the marriage. Instead, we are called to choose submission to each other as a Spirit-filled response that honors Christ. Submission involves the intentional, self-sacrificing effort to be other-centered rather than following our natural inclination to be self-centered. No one exemplifies this more than Christ, who is the supreme example of submission for the good of others.

> Have this mind among yourselves, which is yours in Christ Jesus, who, though he was in the form of God, did not count equality with God a thing to be grasped, but made himself nothing, taking the form of a servant, being born in the likeness of men. And being found in human form, he humbled himself by becoming obedient to the point of death, even death on a cross. (Philippians 2:5-8)

The Greek word *hupotasso* in Ephesians 5:22 is often translated as "submitting to" or "being subject to." According to Thayers Greek Lexicon, this word has two primary uses—a military use and a non-military use. Not surprisingly, the military usage has a connotation of being "subject to" or "to obey" as one who is under the command of another. This meaning is often imposed on the text as supporting masculine authority over women. This application gives credence to the belief that leadership is an intrinsically masculine quality while the fundamental "role" of women is to be submissive and responsive to that leadership.

In contrast, Thayers Greek Lexicon defines the non-military use of *hupotasso* as "a voluntary attitude of giving in, cooperating, assuming responsibility, carrying a burden." *The New Century Version* translates *hupotasso* here in Ephesians 5:22 as *yield* rather than *submit*. *The Contemporary English Version* translates verse 22: "A wife should put her husband first, as she does the Lord." *The Message* reads, "Out of respect for Christ, be courteously reverent to one another. Wives, understand and support your husband in ways that show your support for Christ."

Since the focus of Ephesians 5:21-33 is on love and mutual respect, a better translation of *submit* is *to be supportive of, to adapt to, and to yield to*. There are other compelling reasons why this makes sense. The idea of willingly submitting ourselves to one another is based on our reverence for Christ. As seen in Philippians 2:5-8, Jesus is our example of what submission and leadership looks like. He didn't come as a military leader to command, rule, and give orders to his church. He came as a servant-leader to give his life for us (Mark 10:45). He consistently renounced hierarchy and the idea of "lording" over others (1 Peter 5:3, Mark 10:32). The idea of wives being under the command or control of their husbands contradicts everything Jesus taught about how his Kingdom functions (Matthew 20:25-28, Luke 22:25-27, John 13:2-17).

HEADS UP

That said, the second controversial word is found in the phrase "the husband is head of the wife" (Ephesians 5:23). Here we have another misunderstood term used to support the subordination of women. Two questions must be asked. First, what does the term head really mean? Second, what does the headship of a man look like?

There are multitudes of opinions and scholarly papers on the original meaning of the Greek word *kephalē* (head) used here. In classical Greek, the word typically referred to a person's physical head. In English, the word has many meanings. One metaphorical meaning is leader or chief person, being the head of an organization or top person in its hierarchical structure. It can also refer to source as in the headwaters of a river.

In Koine Greek, the language used in New Testament times, the word *kephalē* also has metaphorical meanings. According to Liddel, Scott, and Jones's Greek-English Lexicon (LSJ), one of the most exhaustive and respected lexicons of ancient Greek, possible meanings are a source, an origin, or a starting point. Neither authority nor leader are listed as possible meanings of *kephalē*.

Christ is the model for all believers (Ephesians 4:13; 4:32-5:2), even as the head, which 4:15-16 explains as being the source of the body's growth.

> Rather, speaking the truth in love, we are to grow up in every way into him who is the head, into Christ, from whom the whole body, joined and held together by every joint with which it is equipped, when each part is working properly, makes the body grow so that it builds itself up in love.

In 5:23, Paul similarly defines what he means by head in equating it with Savior.

> For the husband is the head of the wife even as Christ is the head of the church, his body, and is himself its Savior.

What does Christ do as Savior? Paul goes on to explain this when he describes Christ giving himself up for the church (Ephesians 5:25), nourishing the church, and cherishing it (Ephesians 5:29). That's a Christian husband's job description.

In contrast to this description, many standard lexicons and dictionaries for New Testament Greek define *kephalē* as meaning "authority over." Bauer-Arndt-Gingrich-Danker gives the following definition: "In the case of living beings, [it is used] to denote superior rank."

So which is it? Does it mean "source and origin" or does it mean "chief person and superior rank"? Context is the key to determining how a term, especially one as controversial as this, is used in each passage. Considering the overall context of this passage, it isn't convincing that the meaning being referenced is a husband's superior rank over his wife. Instead, a far more definitive question is how is the meaning of *kephalē* demonstrated? What does it really look like? How does it function in relationship to a husband and wife? Most importantly how was this "headship" modeled for us by Jesus himself?

To answer that question, we need look no further than Ephesians 5:22-33 itself, which gives us the divine pattern for headship. Martyn Lloyd-Jones put it this way in referencing this passage.

> This is the secret – that we are ever to be looking unto him and realizing that marriage is but a pale reflection between Christ and the church.

COUNTER-CULTURAL LOVE

The loving language used in Ephesians 5:21-33 makes it clear that the focus isn't on a mandatory or mechanical arrangement of female submission and male rule. It is instead a radical call to selflessness and unity. We see a counter-cultural love from a husband toward his wife and from a wife toward her husband. Men are to love their wives just like Christ loved the church. and women are to receive that unconditional love as the church receives it from Christ. For a culture where husband/wife roles and relationships were rigidly defined, this was a revolutionary teaching. Submission and headship were part of the patriarchal culture. Paul was introducing the concept of Christ-like love and mutual submission as a reflection of the radical nature of the gospel.

The emphasis in teaching this passage has often been on wives submitting to the superior rank of their husbands. Paul's use of the head-body metaphor points to a dramatically different relationship dynamic. In describing Jesus as the head of the church, which is his body (Ephesians 5:23, 30), Paul is focusing on the unity made possible and maintained because of the demonstration of Christ's love. The church sustains this union by being cooperative and faithful to Jesus. In marriage, the husband (the metaphorical head) and the wife (the metaphorical body) are also to be united. God created the man and the woman and brought them together so that the two would become one. Oneness is identified as the main outcome of that union.

To foster this unity, Paul urges husbands to love their wives "as Christ loved the church and gave himself up for her" (Ephesians 5:25). He further urges husbands to "love their own wives as they love their own bodies" (Ephesians 5:28), adding, "he who loves his wife loves himself. After all, no one ever hated their own body, but they feed and care for their body, just as Christ does the church" (Ephesians 5:28-29).

Nowhere in Ephesians 5 does Paul use the Greek words for leader, ruler, or authority in reference to husbands. In contrast, he uses the word *love* six times when speaking to husbands about how they are to relate to their wives, twice in verse 25, three times in verse 28, and once in verse 31. The ultimate goal of this head/body relationship is love, unity, and oneness.

> Therefore, a man shall leave his father and mother and hold fast to his wife, and the two shall become one flesh. This mystery is profound, and I am saying that it refers to Christ and the church. However, let each one of you love his wife as himself, and let the wife see that she respects her husband. (Ephesians 5:31, 32)

Oneness, unity, and mutual submission are the focus for both husband and wife. Husbands are urged to love and nurture their wives, and wives are urged to be cooperative, and loyal (i.e., submissive), as well as respectful to their husbands (Ephesians 5:22, 33b).

A Significant Error

Unfortunately, when the focal point of this passage is reduced to one phrase, "the husband is the head of the wife," these eight words are isolated to stand on their own like one of the Ten Commandments. This is a significant error. As a viable alternative, the primary emphasis is a living definition of headship as demonstrated by Christ himself. So rather than over-focusing on the technical meaning of head as authority and ruler or as source and origin, we should look at how Christ himself demonstrated *kephalē*.

Regardless of how one chooses to define the word, how it behaves and manifests in real life is far more important. Simply having a correct definition of the word *kephalē* will not give married couples the grace and power to live out a Christ-centered marriage. John Stott explains:

> If headship means power in any sense, then it is power to care, not to crush. Power to serve, not to dominate. Power to facilitate self-fulfillment, not to frustrate or destroy it. And in all this the standard of the husband's love is to be the cross of Christ, on which he surrendered himself even to death in his selfless love for his bride.

In the final analysis of Ephesians 5:21-33, Paul calls both wives and husbands to defer to and nurture one another. We receive the exact same message regarding the mutuality of marriage in Paul's most detailed treatment of the subject in 1 Corinthians 7. Here he specifies the same opportunities and obligations for wives and husbands regarding numerous issues related to marriage, both physical and spiritual. In each, he addresses men and women as equals. His wording is symmetrically balanced to reinforce this equality. Paul affirms that the husband and wife mutually possess each other.

> The wife gives authority over her body to her husband, and the husband gives authority over his body to his wife. (1 Corinthians 7:4)

All of this was part of the revolutionary, counter-cultural lifestyle Paul reveals as the outworking of the gospel message in marriage. In both Ephesians 5 and 1 Corinthians 7, Paul offers a paradigm-shattering vision of marriage as a relationship in which the partners are bonded together in submission to one another and to Christ.

Again, Marg Mowczko, in a blog, *The Priority of Wifely Submission VS. Mutual Submission,* writes:

> A marriage of two competent people simply does not need one person to always be the leader and the other person to always be the submissive follower. In fact, Christian marriages work better without a gender hierarchy. A marriage may not need a leader, but families with young children do. I firmly believe that God's ideal is that families and households be led jointly by parents, where the family responsibilities and resources are shared, not according to rigid gender roles and cultural expectations, but according to each person's skills, abilities and temperaments; where neither the husband nor the wife is "the boss" because the real leader is the Lord Jesus Christ, leading and guiding through the Holy Spirit.

A BETTER WAY

Biblical egalitarian theology is gaining recognition in the mainstream of Christian thinking, and the egalitarian marriage model is more widely accepted. *The New Dictionary of Christian Ethics and Pastoral Theology* defines marriage as a co-partnership of equality where "neither may lord it over the other." This definition clearly characterizes an egalitarian view of marriage with mutuality, a high degree of intimacy, and without forced roles.

So how does an egalitarian marriage look different than a complementarian marriage? How do these differences play out in a couple's relationship? Perhaps using those labels to define marriage really isn't as important as asking the question, "Do we have a biblical marriage?" We (Eric and Carol) believe such a marriage would hold to the following priorities we are committed to in our own relationship.

We are submitted to Jesus as Lord

The ultimate focus of headship and authority in marriage should be centered on Jesus's Lordship. That doesn't mean neither husband or wife may not be tempted to step into the role of "God" from time to time. Before we were married, Jesus was our Lord and the one we committed our lives to follow. Now that we're married, Jesus is still our Lord and is still the one we've committed our lives to follow. The difference now is that we get to figure out what following him together looks like.

We agree to make decisions together

This goes hand-in-hand with having Jesus as *the head*. Jesus leads *both* spouses into a *unified* decision. Neither person has more potential than the other to hear God's guidance based on gender.

God speaks to everyone, providing an unending opportunity for both spouses to seek and hear him. Whatever the circumstance, if a couple doesn't collaborate on a decision, it can create a rift in their relationship that widens over time. On the other hand, a decision made together by a husband and wife is powerful. What we decide together affects who we are becoming and where our marriage is heading.

We submit to one another, seeking the best for our spouse

Jesus is the head to whom both husband and wife should be submitted. In its discussion of marriage, Ephesians 5 speaks specifically about husbands and wives submitting to one another out of reverence for Christ (v. 21). The same passage goes on to describe how the wife is to respect and submit to her husband and how the husband is to demonstrate his respect and submission to his wife by putting her needs before his own.

We commit to growing together and being equally yoked spiritually

Neither spouse uses their level of spiritual maturity to have greater control in the relationship. Marriage is an equal playing field for growth as followers of Jesus. In Jesus's explanations of the Kingdom of God, he uses agricultural metaphors like seeds (Matthew 13, Luke 13), fruit (Matthew 7, Mark 4), wheat (John 12), and a vineyard (John 15). All these metaphors reference a process of growth that occurs when Jesus is honored as the source of life.

Growing individually as well as a couple is a significant indicator that Jesus himself is the head of that marriage.

We mutually esteem each other

Ephesians 5 encourages men, who have traditionally possessed greater physical, social, and economic power, to elevate women to a place of equal standing as fellow members of Christ's body (v. 30). Women have been traditionally viewed as subordinate in marriage, in the church, and most cultures still struggle with giving them equal status with men. Conversely, serious damage is also done to marriages when women disrespect and emasculate their husbands.

At the end of the day, Christian marriage isn't defined by rules, roles, and religion but by a couple's unified pursuit of Jesus as Lord, Savior, and head of his body, the church. While this describes the kind of marriage we always desired to have, we never thought it possible during the years we labored under the constraints of a complementarian relationship. Now that we understand what true biblical marriage looks like, the prospect of knowing greater joy and fulfillment in marriage is no longer a daydream or wishful thinking.

Part IV:

Who Has Compromised?

"And do you not know that you are Eve? God's sentence hangs still over all your sex and his punishment weighs down upon you. You are the devil's gateway."

—Tertullian

"You are a chosen people, royal priesthood, a holy nation, God's special possession, that you may declare the praises of him who called you out of darkness into his wonderful light."

—the Apostle Peter

Chapter Twenty-Two

The Things that Matter

Martin Luther King, Jr. once said, "Our lives begin to end the day we become silent about things that matter." For this very reason, it is urgent that we speak up and have this crucial conversation with our brothers and sisters in Christ.

We must also continue to ask crucial questions. How can there possibly be gender equality if men are given authority over women? How can women be denied leadership roles when the Old and New Testaments affirm God's calling on both men and women? How can gender-based hierarchy possibly represent God's divine order when the New Testament affirms mutual submission and respect? How can the church sanction male dominance and even superiority when ethnic and gender disparity were eliminated at the cross?

These questions represent just a few of the inconsistencies of complementarian doctrine. And the stakes for this crucial conversation are high. Above all because of the enormous possibilities and opportunities that such a serious dialogue and reflection could generate, including:

- Living more closely to how God intended; displaying God's glory more accurately as male and female.

- Removing unnecessary stumbling blocks to Christianity and the gospel.

- Safeguarding against abuse and gender discrimination.

- Setting an example of equality and mutuality within the global church.

- Enabling the full expression of God-given gifts and callings so the church can continue to grow and mature.

- Creating accountability often missing in male dominated church leadership.

Coram Deo

The Latin phrase *Coram Deo* refers to living before the face of God so that his is the only face or opinion that matters. Such is the commitment indispensable for anyone attempting to dialogue on a topic that is both controversial and sacred. The role of women in the church and home certainly fits those criteria. It became apparent the morning I (Carol) began writing on this subject that I myself needed a renewed commitment to live Coram Deo in order to resist self-censorship due to a fear of rejection.

The morning I began writing this book on gender justice, I awoke from an unsettling if not uncommon dream. You may have experienced it—the one where you are in the public's eye and realize you don't have any clothes on. In my dream, a full-blown panic ensued as I looked around for something to cover myself. Not finding any of my own clothes, I attempted to borrow someone else's. If that wasn't traumatic enough, my dad showed up, escalating my sense of shame.

In my dream, I was anticipating my dad's stern disapproval. To my surprise, he wasn't upset with me but with those who seemed to be relishing my vulnerability. He addressed by name two pastors known for their hardline stance against women leaders in the church. My dad could see I was emotionally imploding under their censure. Rather than being there to reprimand me, my dad was there to protect me.

Thankfully, at that point I woke up to the welcomed realization it was only a dream. Embolden by my dad's support, even if in a dream, I took my first baby steps to pen fifty-thousand words during a thirty-day writing challenge. I had been greatly impacted by Dan Kimball's book, *They like Jesus But Not the Church*, which presents six common objections emerging generations have about the church and Christianity. One chapter is titled, "The Church is Dominated by Males and Oppresses Females." In it, Kimball addresses the negative reputation of the church as being "a boys club."

Of all the topics covered, this was the most likely to garner criticism, and Kimball candidly confesses his own physical and emotional angst as he wrote and his relief when the chapter was finished. Though he describes himself as one who "avoids confrontation and dreads having to dispute anything," he courageously starts this book with the phrase: "The world has changed. Don't be weaklings!"

Kimball's words have resonated with Eric and me during the arduous journey of writing this book. It would have been easy to allow the controversial nature of gender equality to derail our quest for more satisfying biblical answers. As we've heard a similar theme emerging from many sectors of Christianity, we've been heartened to recognize there is a compelling case to be made in support for the women's movement in the church.

With twenty-first century western culture making sexual identity a matter of choice, it is more important than ever for believers to have a clear grasp of what the Bible teaches about manhood and womanhood. Complementarians often present doomsday scenarios for any deviation from their ideology. Complementarians claim to have launched a counter-cultural defense of the biblical position in opposition to what they reference derogatorily as Christian feminism. The reality is that patriarchal theology is not counter-cultural. It has been the ruling norm in every country and culture since our world was infected by sin as Satan set up his reign of terror.

It is hard not to relate sympathetically to the outrage directed at the church from the modern-day feminist movement. Much of this movement has been a response to the tyranny and oppression of patriarchy that has shaped world history as well as the church. The very church that should have been proclaiming the value, dignity, and equality of women as modeled by Jesus chose instead to betray them. Rather than protecting women, the church has often been complicit in supporting the mistreatment of women. The very scriptures that declare a woman's value and equality to men as God's image-bearers have been used to depreciate them.

In contrast, the real counter-cultural movement began through the example of Jesus and the early church, establishing a restored Kingdom culture of equality for both men and women under the New Covenant. Sadly, that Kingdom culture was largely lost in the centuries that followed. The time has come for a new reformation on the church's view of women.

Pandora's Box

The issue of women's equality in the church has long been considered a Pandora's Box, never to be opened. Who was Pandora? The original myth of Pandora's Box was a kind of a theodicy, addressing the question of why there is evil in the world. Not unlike many church fathers, the ancient Greeks blamed women for the world's suffering. According to the myth, Pandora was the first human woman created. Each of the Greek gods gave her a unique gift, but the gifts were all evil, such as sickness, war, suffering, pain, death. So she was given a special box to contain the gifts with instructions never to open it. Overcome by curiosity, she opens the box releasing all its evils into the world.

There are two renditions of how this story ends. In one, Pandora is so horrified by what she's done that she slams the lid, trapping the final gift of hope so it is unavailable to mortal men. In the other version, hope escapes before the lid shuts, giving humanity the prospect at least of overcoming evil. Both versions have influenced Jewish and Christian theology, perpetuating a misogynous view of women.

As with Pandora, the mere discussion of a woman's role in church leadership has been viewed as somehow opening a "box" to all kinds of evil, unraveling the moral fabric of society. A handful of Bible verses are used to keep the "lid" slammed on women's involvement in influential leadership roles. In so doing, is it possible that hope is also being held hostage?

What is certain is that we are seeing a change. Biblical scholars, respected pastors, seminary professors, even influential conservative voices are bringing this topic out into the mainstream of Christianity for discussion. Pastors of local churches are re-examining the Bible, only to find the witness of Scripture affirming women as pastors and teachers. Even within the evangelical movement, women are being endorsed as leaders where they were once unwelcome.

As we bring our discussion to a close, we believe the Pandora's Box analogy takes on a different story line. Without sounding too dramatic or inflammatory, Pandora's Box has already been opened, unleashing on the world a social system called patriarchy. A system intended by Satan to oppress and antagonize the woman and "her seed." We also know all hope was not lost and that from the beginning God had already set in motion his rescue plan.

Chapter Twenty-Three

What's the Point?

The church has often unwisely assumed the position of God in defining and dictating exactly what it means to be masculine or feminine. Isn't God the potter and we the clay? If I (Carol) were a betting woman, I would wager some of the narrow, confining definitions of womanhood and manhood have significantly contributed to a sense of self-rejection for many men and women. Who are we to say what is fit and unfit when determining God's handiwork and design (Ephesians 2:10)? How a woman expresses herself may look very different from other women as well as from images of femininity formed in childhood. The same thing is true for men.

The concern expressed that a departure from a complementarian model of womanhood and manhood automatically leads to gender blending is simply not the case. The idea that egalitarian principles inherently support radical feminism within the church is unsubstantiated. Ironically, the egalitarian model more faithfully supports biblical characteristics of what a complementary relationship looks like, i.e., a relationship that fashions individual roles to fit each other's unique God-given design. This in turn promotes a relationship that can truly complement and complete each other.

I get nervous when I see church leaders, the majority being men, forming a cohort to define what biblical manhood and womanhood must look like. This is precisely what the Council for Biblical Manhood and Womanhood is doing. Our concern is that men and women who ascribe to their dictates and those set forth in their manifesto, "Recovering Manhood and Womanhood," are letting others define who they are, what they can and cannot do, and how they are to express themselves even at the cost of their true identity as Kingdom citizens. The church has been notorious for its attempts to control the sanctification process through conformity. This is just one more example of the heavy hand of religion.

In truth, it is the Holy Spirit who oversees "just as he determines" (1 Corinthians 12:11) the distribution of gifts and roles that equip each of us uniquely to serve God. The beauty of biblical egalitarianism is that each man and woman is invited to discover their gifts, then entrusted with the proper use of these gifts to advance God's Kingdom (Romans 12:1-8). In consequence, a biblical egalitarian marriage relationship will take on the unique shape of two individuals coming together as one. Both will lead in their strengths and follow in their support of each other as they learn mutual submission and servanthood.

No Iron-Clad Expectations!

Eric and I are not advocating for equal rights based on a subjective sense of fairness but on sound biblical and historical accounts that open doors of opportunity for women to walk through. Both men and women need to be encouraged and trained in order to fulfill their calling. Obviously, not all women are called to be leaders and teachers, but some are. I (Carol) remember one young woman holding back the tears while sharing her fear of becoming a pastor's wife. I had been her main model of what a pastor's wife looked like (no wonder she felt like crying!). She just couldn't imagine ever doing what I did in that role.

I was able to reassure her that she didn't have to be like me and vice versa. Although different from mine, her spiritual gifts had been very effective in serving the church and would be equally needed in partnership with her husband.

We must never lose sight of how uniquely God created men and women as well as the uniqueness expressed in each gender. With egalitarian theology, there are no ironclad extra-biblical expectations of what every man or woman is to do or to be like. In marriage, a husband and wife can develop different partnership styles that best utilize their gifts and design, including roles that might be characterized as complementarian. Since complementarian theology is ridged and pre-formatted, this unfortunately precludes any such flexibility or adaptability.

A Challenge to Women

Eric and I have an ultimate objective in mind—that the Christian community would become a far more dynamic representation of the Kingdom of God in which women are given their rightful place alongside men as God's image-bearers. The church should be a safe place where relationships broken by sin and the curse are restored, and unity prevails over division and discrimination. There is nowhere on earth such a reality could exist except where Jesus is Lord. J. Lee Gray in his book *Fearless Daughters of the Bible* states:

> The conservative American church has conditioned women to be passive. For years we have told women to be quiet and to wait for men to give them instructions. Meanwhile, the Holy Spirit has been wooing women to tune out the voice of religion so they can hear His voice.

Gray's statement addresses the problem while also expressing the same hope we feel. Anne Graham Lotz, daughter of the late Billy Graham, adds to this:

> The very first person to be commissioned was a woman. And she was commissioned to go to men to share her testimony . . . and then also to give his [Jesus] Word. I know there are some people who will draw a line and say I can give a testimony, but I can't share the Scripture. But Jesus didn't make that distinction. He gave Mary Magdalene both commissions, to share her testimony and to give out his Word (John 20:18).

The Kingdom of God needs more women of vision and courage to move out of their comfort zone and take a more prominent role in God's epic story. This will look different for each woman. But it requires the same thing from all of us—a greater passion to grow in our unique expression of God's image. The Kingdom of God is moving forward, and we must be willing to move forward with it. For some, that means helping to lead the movement.

When teaching classes on the priesthood of the believer, I (Carol) emphasize how every Christian has a calling to serve. Whether you are a man or a woman, membership in the priesthood is the common ground that brings all believers together as ministers. In several classes, I had students from religious backgrounds where only select men could serve as priests. The biblical concept of each believer being part of the priesthood came to them as a real surprise. Some were reluctant to change their mindset to embrace such a concept. I have also heard similar objections from Protestant brothers and sisters. My observation is that many believers don't want to take the full responsibility of such a weighty position. They prefer letting the professionals do the work of ministry as Bible teachers and spiritual leaders.

Ladies, you may very well feel the same way when considering what it means to take your place of equal partnership with men (Genesis 1:27, 28). We understand that not all women are leaders, but we are all ministers. And we are hopeful that more women will respond to the call to leadership in the church and that the church will embrace them. As a woman, you are a God-given gift to the body of Christ. As you find your voice to speak with greater boldness, the church will become a more robust representation of the body and bride of Christ.

A Challenge to Men and the Church

Is God trying to speak to his church and more specifically to its male contingent? If so, are we (Eric now speaking here!) listening to the right voice? Here are some statements from prominent leaders of the present-day Christian patriarchy movement. Do they appear to represent the voice of God or a display of patriarchal chauvinism?

James A. Fowler: Women in the Church, 1999

Fowler, speaking on behalf of God, uses twenty-five remarkably condescending terms listing every obnoxious trait and behavior often used to depict women within patriarchy. This he does to call for the subordination of women in the home, church, and society and to justify paternalism as necessary to protect women from themselves.

> The Holiness of God is not evidenced in women when they are brash, brassy, boisterous, brazen, head-strong, strong-willed, loud-mouthed, overly-talkative, having to have the last word, challenging, controlling, manipulative, critical, conceited, arrogant, aggressive, assertive, strident, interruptive, undisciplined, insubordinate, disruptive, dominating, domineering, or clamoring for power. Rather, women accept God's holy order and character by being humbly and

unobtrusively respectful and receptive in functional subordination to God, church leadership, and husbands.

OWEN STRACHAN, EXECUTIVE DIRECTOR OF THE COUNCIL OF BIBLICAL MANHOOD AND WOMANHOOD

Strachan believes that men must exercise authority over women and that the fall of humanity was caused by Eve not maintaining her proper place in submission to Adam.

> Yet God made the man first, and he gives Adam a leadership role by asking him to exercise authority over the animals by naming them . . . Everything falls apart in the fall. Adam fails to lead and protect Eve. Eve is deceived by the serpent and assumes the role of leader (Genesis 3:1-13). In short, the fall itself involves an inversion of God's plans for men and women.

BRUCE WARE, PROFESSOR OF CHRISTIAN THEOLOGY, SOUTHERN BAPTIST THEOLOGICAL SEMINARY

Ware believes women demonstrate whether they are in fact Christian by submitting to male authority and embracing the roles of wife and mother.

> It means that a woman will demonstrate that she is in fact a Christian, that she has submitted to God's ways by affirming and embracing her God-designed identity as—for the most part, generally this is true—as wife and mother, rather than chafing against it, rather than bucking against it, rather than wanting to be a man, wanting to be in a man's position, wanting to teach and exercise authority over men.

JOHN PIPER, LEADER OF THE GOSPEL COALITION

Piper promotes the idea that a mature woman will affirm, receive, and nurture the strength and leadership of men in all her relationships with men. To not do so controverts God's created order. He believes that the church is to reflect a masculine Christianity.

> To the degree that a woman's influence over man is personal and directive it will generally offend a man's good, God-given sense of responsibility and leadership, and thus controvert God's created order. A woman may design the traffic pattern of a city's streets and thus exert a kind of influence over all male drivers. But this influence will be non-personal and therefore not necessarily an offense against God's order . . . Similarly in the workplace it may not be nonsense in any given circumstance for a woman to provide a certain kind of direction for a man, but to do it in such a way that she signals her endorsement of his unique duty as a man to feel a responsibility of strength and protection and leadership toward her as a woman and toward women in general . . . God has made Christianity to have a masculine feel. He has ordained for the church a masculine ministry. He does not intend for women to languish or be frustrated or in any way suffer or fall short of full and lasting joy in this masculine Christianity, from which I infer that the fullest flourishing of women and men takes place in churches and families that have this masculine feel.

John MacArthur, Senior Pastor, Grace Community Church

MacArthur believes that no biblical case can be made for a woman preacher, even one who is teaching other women, including Beth Moore, who he told "Go home!" He continued his public renunciation of her and all women preacher/teachers to a cheering crowd of men by saying:

> Just because you have the skill to sell jewelry on the TV sales channel doesn't mean you should be preaching... When the leaders of evangelicalism roll over for women preachers, the feminists have really won the battle . . . they want power, not equality.

Mark Driscoll, Founder of Mars Hill Nondenominational Mega-Church Franchise

Driscoll is known for his blatantly misogynistic comments and teaching regarding women.

> Women will be saved by going back to that role that God has chosen for them. Ladies, if the hair on the back of your neck stands up it is because you are fighting your role in the Scripture.

Frankly, when I (Eric) read quotes like those above, it's the hair on the back of my own neck that stands up. Although I deeply admire these men as Christian brothers, such displays of conventional masculine arrogance are unfortunately far too common in the complementarian movement, exposing the spirit behind its condescending position. I have concluded that any teaching that promotes the superior status of men invites the ugly face of patriarchy to find expression in the church. I believe this is a tragic misrepresentation of the Gospel to a watching world.

Epilogue

Setting the Record Straight

What we see in Scripture and history is the epic story of God restoring the relationship of his image-bearers to true oneness. From Genesis to Revelation, this expression of God's Kingdom on earth has been moving toward the reinstatement of redeemed men and women as co-rulers of this Kingdom. Modeled by Jesus himself, the dignity and respect women received in the early church was a revolutionary movement unparalleled by any other religion, culture, and time in history.

So why was such a beautiful display of God's Kingdom on earth abandoned? Have we now arrived at another pivotal moment in time? Are we once again strategically positioned to influence culture and society by supporting women to take their rightful place alongside men in the renewal of the church? Or is the church going to lag and continue to hinder women from exercising the gifts and callings that are part of their God-given heritage?

Proponents of Christian patriarchy claim that any other position on women in ministry and marriage undermines the authority of Scripture. There are three assumptions with this reasoning that we (Eric and Carol) find to be faulty. First, it assumes biblical egalitarianism is in alignment with a worldview that opposes Christianity. Secondly, it assumes egalitarians have adopted their biblical view as a result of cultural pressure coming from a secular viewpoint. Thirdly, it disregards the biblical scholarship of countless renowned Christian theologians and scholars who support an egalitarian position.

In speaking about gospel unity, Dr. Gerry Breshears, Professor of Theology at Western Seminary, believes it should be based on what he calls Levels of Certainty. In other words, Christians should keep the main thing the main thing. He sums it up like this:

> Wise Christians understand that some issues, which may seem fundamental, are actually seeds of division planted by the enemy of our souls.

How true that statement is when it comes to egalitarian versus complementarian convictions. In determining which battles to fight and how fiercely, Dr. Breshears suggests a "Four D" model. I.e., as Christians there are things to DIE FOR, things to DIVIDE FOR, things to DEBATE FOR, and things to DECIDE FOR.

Let's look at each in context of the egalitarian-complementarian discussion. First, few people would take the position to DIE FOR this issue. Other than character assassinations, no one has yet taken it that far. Though for some, the very level of animosity reveals a chauvinistic sexism hiding behind a biblical façade.

Sadly, the unfortunate choice of many is to DIVIDE FOR this issue. While disappointing, it represents the freedom we have in the pursuit of truth.

It is our prayer that more people who disagree on this subject will be open to DEBATE FOR. The Bible says that "iron sharpens iron" (Proverbs 27:17), and such discussions can be of tremendous benefit for those on either side of this issue.

And in the end, we can all thank God we're at liberty to DECIDE FOR! Our hope is that whatever one's position on women in leadership in the church and home, both sides can agree to disagree agreeably. Rupertus Meldenius is credited with this well-known Christian dictum: "In essentials unity. In non-essentials liberty. In all things charity."

We believe there is a growing awareness in the Christian community of how the gospel liberates women from restrictions still being imposed by the church. We believe that God is speaking. It might be more accurate to say that God is reminding us of what he has already said. In Joel 2:28-29 and again in Acts 2:1-18 (GNT), we read these prophetic words:

> This is what I will do in the last days, God says: I will pour out my Spirit on everyone. Your sons and daughters will proclaim my message; your young men will see visions, and your old men will have dreams. Yes, even on my servants, both men and women, I will pour out my Spirit in those days, and they will proclaim my message.

This passage clearly shows God's intended purpose to be gender inclusive and not exclusive. No one is to be left out or limited from representing him and speaking on his behalf. Sons and daughters, men and women, young and old, servants and freemen will be used to proclaim the good news without discrimination. In fact, it echoes Paul's description in Galatians of the oneness we have in Christ where there is no distinction or division based on race, status, or gender.

> There is neither Jew nor Gentile, neither slave nor free, nor is there male and female, for you are all one in Christ Jesus. (Galatians 3:28)

From the very beginning, God's heart can be seen in the oneness and mutuality of his image-bearers. True manhood and womanhood can be found there. Although lost to the devasting consequences of sin and buried under the crushing weight of patriarchy, our true identities have been restored through the gospel and saving grace of our Lord Jesus Christ. God's story, a progressive revelation of his redemptive plan written on the pages of Scripture and incarnated in the lives of courageous men and women, challenges each of us to reclaim all that it means to be created in his image as it was "from the beginning."

About the Authors

Eric Scott Smith holds a Masters in Global Leadership from Western Seminary and has been in pastoral ministry for forty-five years, including thirty-one years as lead teaching pastor of South Valley Community Church in Gilroy, California.

Carol Nelson-Smith also served on the ministerial staff of the church as well as teaching on leadership and ministry development.

Eric and Carol travel extensively to train church leadership in developing countries. They are both authors and bloggers on their ministry website youdefineus.org. The Smiths have three children and three grandchildren.

You can contact Eric and Carol at **www.youdefineus.org**.

Made in the USA
San Bernardino, CA
14 May 2020